Current Issues
In Business and Economics
Number One

The Department of Economics is pleased to collaborate with the Business Research and Service Institute in presenting this symposium in which five distinguished economists discuss the issues of economic freedom, stability and growth.

Current Issues
In Business and Economics
Number One

Economic Freedom, Stability and Growth

Department of Economics
Western Michigan University

Business Research and Service Institute
College of Business
Western Michigan University

PREFACE

In the winter and spring of 1971, five distinguished economists were invited to the campus of Western Michigan University
to conduct seminars on the issues of economic freedom, stability,
and growth. The five papers included here are based on the presentations made at the seminar sessions.

The Topics

Each speaker addresses himself to a topic in his special field
of interest, and together they cover a wide range of issues. Profes-
sors David Fand and James M. Buchanan devote full attention to
domestic problems of this country. Professor Gardner Ackley dis-
cusses international inflation. Professor Harry G. Johnson presents
a model of economic growth for less developed countries and
Professor Martin Bronfenbrenner explains the postwar economic
progress of Japan.

This symposium serves the purpose of bringing to the readers
examinations of a variety of current economic problems. More
importantly, this is a series of seminars on macroeconomic theory
and policy. All the speakers are fundamentally economic theorists.
It is hoped that the reader will understand from this series of lectures how macroeconomic theory is applied to current issues and
in what ways the theory is relevant to the world's economic
problem.

The Speakers

The five speakers come from the East and West coasts as well as from
the Midwest, and represent a wide spectrum of opinion in academic circles.

PROFESSOR DAVID FAND of Wayne State University has written exten-
sively on the subject of monetary policy. His most recent publications are "A
Monetarist Model of the Monetary Process" in the May, 1970 issue of the
Journal of Finance, and "Monetarism and Fiscalism" in the September, 1970
issue of the *Bance Nazionale Del Lavare Quarterly Review.* Dr. Fand has

served as consultant to the Joint Economic Committee, the Department of Commerce, the Department of Treasury, the Small Business Administration and the Board of Governors of the Federal Reserve System. He is a member of the editorial board of the *Journal of Economic Literature* and a member of the advisory board of the *Journal of Money, Credit and Banking.*

PROFESSOR JAMES M. BUCHANAN is Director of the Center for Study of Public Choice at Virginia Polytechnic Institute and State University, Blacksburg, Virginia. At the time of the seminar, he was a visiting professor at the University of California at Los Angeles. Professor Buchanan is a member of President Nixon's Task Force on Model Cities. He has written several books on public finance and economic policy. His publications include *Calculus of Consent,* (1962), co-authored with Professor Gordon Tullock. His most recent books are *Cost and Choice: An Inquiry in Theory,* (1969), and *Academia in Anarchy: An Economic Theory,* (1970), with Professor Nices E. Devletoglou. Professor Buchanan has held office in several professional organizations. He was President of the Southern Economic Association in 1963, the co-founder of the Public Choice Society in 1963, a member of the Executive Committee of the American Economic Association from 1966 to 1969, and is now a vice president of that organization.

PROFESSOR GARDNER ACKLEY, of the University of Michigan, was chairman of the Council of Economic Advisors from 1964 to 1968. He was the Ambassador to Italy from 1968 to 1969. In addition, he has served with many government agencies including the National Resources Planning Board, the Office of Price Administration, and the Office of Strategic Services. Professor Ackley served as a member of the editorial board of the *American Economic Review* from 1953 to 1956, and was a director of the Social Science Research Council from 1959 to 1961.

PROFESSOR HARRY G. JOHNSON is now concurrently Professor of Economics at the University of Chicago and the London School of Economics and Political Science. He has published numerous books and articles in the fields of international trade, monetary theory, and economic development. Among his publications are the following: *The World Economy at the Cross Road,* (1965); *Economic Nationalism in Old and New States,* (1967); *Economic Policies Toward Less Developed Countries,* (1967); and *Harmonization of National Economic Policies under Free Trade,* (1967).

PROFESSOR MARTIN BRONFENBRENNER was at Carnegie-Mellon University at the time of the seminar. He is now Professor of Economics at Duke University. He has published widely in professional journals on subjects such as income distribution, monetary-fiscal policies, and the Japanese economy. His most recent books are: *Is the Business Cycle Obsolete?,* (1969), and *Income Distribution Theory,* (1971). Professor Bronfenbrenner was a member of the editorial board of the *American Economic Review* from 1961 to 1964, and is a member of the editorial boards of *Southern Economic Journal, Trans-action,* and *History of Political Economy.*

The Editing
Editing has been done with the objective of bringing out the main ideas

PREFACE

of the seminars. Re-writing was kept to a minimum to preserve the direct, informal and lively presentation of the speakers. Because the presentations were made in the atmosphere of a seminar where the speakers and the audience were exploring new ideas and new approaches to controversial current issues, we must allow our speakers the privilege of presenting tentative observations as well as clear cut conclusions. In many areas under discussion, final conclusions had not yet evolved.

The editorial task was a joint effort with each member of the 1970-1971 Committee on Seminars and Lectures of the Department of Economics of Western Michigan University responsible for editing one paper. Professor Fand's paper was edited by Professor Raymond Zelder, Professor Buchanan's paper by Professor Frank Emerson, Professor Ackley's paper by Professor Myron Ross, Professor Johnson's paper by Professor Wayland Gardner, and Professor Bronfenbrenner's paper by Professor Alfred K. Ho.

Acknowledgement

Recognition is due to the faculty members and students of the Department of Economics of Western Michigan University for their support and cooperation in making the presentation of the seminars possible. Our special thanks go to Dr. Cornelius Loew, Dean of the College of Arts and Sciences, and Professor Robert S. Bowers, Head of the Department of Economics, for arranging the financial support for the seminar and lecture series. We are grateful to Professor James C. Stam, Director of the Business Research and Service Institute, to his staff, and to Mrs. Em Hollingshead and Mrs. Cress Strand of the Department of Economics for their assistance in editing and typing the manuscript.

The Committee on Seminars and Lecturers,

Myron Ross
Raymond Zelder
Wayland Gardner
Frank Emerson
Alfred K. Ho (Chairman)

Kalamazoo, Michigan
September 1971

CONTENTS

INTEREST RATES: AN ECONOMIC THERMOMETER

DAVID FAND

I have selected the subject of interest rates for this seminar because bond yields reached, in 1970, the highest levels since the founding of the republic. The public is greatly concerned with the upward spiral of interest rates, raising long-term rates on new issues of high-grade corporate bonds over 400 basis points—from less than 5% in 1965 to over 9% in 1969. The further back we go in history, the greater is the uncertainty about comparability of data. Nevertheless, for the United Kingdom, where we can obtain interest rate data for a longer period, we find that recent interest rates are the highest recorded since 1727; for the United States, we find that the 1970 rates are the highest recorded since 1800. So, we are now living in a period that is unique in our financial history.

Since there are many interest rates, I shall focus on the highest quality corporate bonds, similar to Aaa corporates today, where the yields typically range from 3½ % to 5%. Sometimes, as in the 1930's, they go down to 3%, or even less, and at other times, i.e. the period following World War I, they may get up as high as 6%. Long-term rates were around 6½ % at the time of the Civil War, and fell below 4% by 1890, reaching a low of 3.3% in 1900. At the end of World War I, they rose again to a peak rate of close to 6%. In 1970, interest rates on new issues of Aaa corporates went above 9%, exceeding the peak rates previously recorded.

Going back to the Civil War, we find that long-term rates normally move in the 3½ % to 5% range, if we exclude the three decades 1929-1959 when bond yields fell below 3%. In the 1880's, long-term rates fell below 4% and did not reach this level

1

again until the beginning of World War I. In the 1920's, long-term rates rose above 5% for some time, but all these examples are small aberrations.

The interest rate chart looks like a temperature chart of a country. When a country is healthy, when things are relatively stable, interest rates are stable and move within the 3½%-5% range. But when a country is not healthy, when it, like a patient, is running a fever, interest rates go way out of line. Thus the interest rate chart appears to reflect the well-being of a country—like a temperature chart reflects the health of an individual.

We have excluded the three decades 1929-1959 because the interest rate movements in this period are most unusual and require separate analysis. From 1930 until 1946, a decade and a half, interest rates were falling almost continuously; and, in 1946, we have the lowest recorded interest rates in the U.S. financial history; the rate on high-grade corporates fell as low as 2.1%. Following this period of declining rates, the U.S. experienced a steady climb back to about the normal range by 1960.

For about five years, from 1959 to 1964, interest rate movements were in the normal range. Starting in 1965, the escalation of interest rates *pari-passu* with the accelerating inflation represents another very unusual chapter in our financial history.

This brief sketch suggests that our interest rate experience in the past four decades is a succession of aberrations, except for possibly a few years in the late fifties and early sixties. The average adult today doesn't know what it means to live in a world of "normal" interest rates because he has never experienced it.

The period starting with 1929, when interest rates were just plummeting down, was the period of the Great Depression, when there was a great loss of confidence in the economy and some economists were enunciating stagnation theories. In the 1930's, the economy was viewed as suffering from arteriosclerosis and stagnation. There was simply no hope. It is an interesting paradox that the theories of economic maturity were being enunciated at the very time that we were entering the age of atomic energy, the nuclear reactor, and the computer—perhaps the most dramatic scientific discoveries in modern history. All these discoveries were just about to burst upon us at the very time when the death sentence of stagnation was being pronounced on the American economy.

The Three Generations

The singular interest rate movements in the past forty years help illustrate the divergence in basic attitudes among various groups. The people who are over fifty, the parents of today's young, are the children who grew to maturity in the 1930's. They are the depression babies: a job was the most important thing to get; and if you had a job, you were among the luckiest people in the world. And these attitudes still tend to be a characteristic of many adults in the over-fifty category who grew up in that period. In contrast, the people who are under thirty, whose experiences and outlook reflect the accelerating inflation of the 1960's, came to believe that jobs are a dime a dozen, because they grew up in an era of excess demand and tight labor market.[1]

The attitudes of these two groups reflect their immediate experience. The over-fifty group is faithful to the Great Depression, and basic attitudes take a long time to change. To illustrate: it took a long period before interest rates returned to normal range from their low point in 1946, presumably because, once people became convinced that they were living in a stagnant economy, it took time before they would change their minds. Similarly, the under-thirty group, who grew up in the 1960's, are tuned in to an inflationary environment.

Three distinct generations may be seen in the public arena at this time. First, we have the generation that grew up in the 1930's, concerned about unemployment, about the GNP, and about jobs, and whose weltanschauung was formulated in the 1930's. We have a second generation that grew up in the early postwar era, say, the fifteen years after World War II, when jobs were still scarce but obtainable. In terms of attitudes and perceptions, this is a moderate, or centrist, group. And, then, we have a third generation—the generation of the 1960's that grew up at a time when finding a job was really no problem, and who, when they quit one job, were able to find another job waiting. This group grew up in the era of the Vietnam escalation, an era of racial conflict and social fragmentation, an era of permissiveness, characterized by experimentation and social engineering. The traumatic upheavals of the 1960's inevitably had a great impact in shaping their "Mod" attitudes.

Perhaps one can now understand why the first generation, the over-fifty group now in position of power, articulates a social philosophy that reflects its upbringing as depression babies. They were just reaching maturity and were badly scarred when the U.S. suffered through the Great Depression. But the fate of the third generation—the under-thirty group—may be even crueler, because its experiences may lead it to believe that everything is possible.

This group reached maturity in a period which was most bizarre, as the interest rate "fever" chart since 1965 would suggest. The second generation, the in-between group, grew up in a more normal period, that left less of an indelible mark on its personality. It is out of sympathy with the "everything-is-possible" approach of the 1960's generation and with the attitudes and philosophy of the depression generation. It is fascinating to realize that a chart of interest rate movements illustrates so faithfully the changing realities of the past four decades.

The Gibson Paradox: High Prices and High Interest Rates

A major analytical issue is involved in interpreting the interest rate behavior known in economic literature as the Gibson Paradox, named after the English writer who first described it. Gibson found, in his studies of financial history, that interest rates and prices are positively correlated—that there is a positive association between high prices and high interest rates. To explain why this condition is paradoxical, consider the following two paradigms of interest rates and prices: in one view, we think of interest rates as causing price level movements so, it follows that low rates should be associated with high prices and high interest rates should be associated with low prices. This approach to interest rates and prices is associated with Wicksell and Keynesian income—expenditure model. But, a monetarist would look at the relation between interest rates and prices somewhat differently, suggesting that *rising* prices should be associated with *high* interest rates. Thus, if everybody knows that prices are rising at 5% a year, the inflation rate will get tacked onto the nominal interest rate. Conversely, *falling* prices should be associated with *low* rates.

Why is the positive association between interest rates and prices a paradox from the monetarist perspective? If prices are rising at a 5% rate per year, then we expect interest rates to be 5% higher than they would otherwise be. However, if prices are high *but no longer rising,* then interest rates should return to their normal level. In other words, interest rates reflect the inflation rate so long as prices are rising; but once prices stop rising, the interest rate should no longer incorporate an inflation premium. For example, if inflation proceeds at a 5% rate for ten years, prices will rise by over 50%. But a price level that is 50% higher but no longer rising should not be associated with *high* interest rates but with *stable* interest rates. In the monetarist view, there is an association between *rising* prices and *high* interest rates but not between *high* prices and *high* interest rates.

Consider now the Gibson Paradox from the Wicksell-Keynes approach which treats interest rates as the cause of prices. If you take this position, you should expect to find *low* rates associated with *high* prices and *high* rates with *low* prices, rather than the association of *high* prices and *high* rates and of *low* prices and *low* rates. The empirical findings highlighted in the Gibson Paradox do not seem to fit either of the two views.[2]

The Keynes-Wicksell Approach: Money, Interest Rates and Prices

Rationalization of the Gibson Paradox may be developed for both the income-expenditure (Wicksellian-Keynesian) and the monetarist (Fisherian) viewpoints. Those viewing interest rates as the cause of prices would explain the association of high rates and high prices by pointing to autonomous forces generating a boom in the real economy which is causing both interest rates and prices to be high. The high interest rates which result from this boom are nevertheless a depressive factor on spending and prevent an even more inflationary situation. Thus, the positive association does not mean that prices are high because interest rates are high. Indeed, prices are high *in spite of* high interest rates and not because of them. It is a *deus ex machina* kind of explanation, but it is one way to explain the paradox.

The Fisher Approach: Money, Prices and Interest Rates

Fisher tries to rationalize the paradox, starting with the alternative idea that prices are the cause of interest rates. He assumes that market interest rates reflect the inflation rate. Fisher then adds another assumption—that the impact of the inflation rate on interest rates is given by a distributed lag—to explain why interest rates remain high even after prices have stopped rising. Fisher contended that these lags are distributed for periods of ten years, fifteen years, or longer.

Fisher's theory is that high rates of monetary growth result in rising prices and that rising prices, in turn, cause high interest rates. But there are lags both in the effects of money on prices and in the effects of prices on interest rates. The observed association of high prices and high interest rates reflects the lag structure of these effects.

The *Mutatis-Mutandis* Effect: Easy Money, Tight Credit and High Rates

The Fisher explanation of the Gibson Paradox has an interesting application in explaining why *high* rates of monetary growth are associated with *high* interest rates. The initial tendency, even among trained economists, is to expect that more, not less, money will tend to lower interest rates. Yet, the historical time-series evidence and the cross-section evidence suggest that the countries with easy money have high interest rates. This evidence seems to suggest that *easy* money leads to *tight* credit and *high* interest rates; and that *tight* money leads to *easy* credit and *low* interest rates.

The Keynesian *Ceteris-Paribus* Liquidity Effect

To rationalize this evidence, we need to distinguish between a *ceteris-paribus* effect—which does not allow for feedback from the real economy—and a *mutatis-mutandis* effect which does. The statement that easier money will cause interest rates to fall is true, if all other factors are equal. But, one must consider whether all factors will stay equal. If they do not, if easier money is going to cause other factors to change, then interest rates may well end up higher.

The historical association of *high* rates of monetary growth with *high* interest rates doesn't mean that the Keynesian liquidity-preference theory is incorrect, but rather that it is an incomplete theory. It is a short-run theory that is appropriate only for particular conditions. The liquidity-preference theory is valid so long as we keep *ceteris-paribus* conditions in mind.[3]

The important question is how the theory is used. Moving along the liquidity-preference curve, we must consider whether this will cause an expansion of income and a rise in prices. The expansion of income will increase the demand for money, and the price rise will reduce the stock of real balances. Looking at the historical record, it would appear that these feedback effects do occur. Consequently, in the *mutatis-mutandis* sense, the surest way to produce low interest rates is to have tight money. The positive association between money and interest is manifest when all factors are taken into account, not just the initial effect.

The *mutatis-mutandis* view does not deny the Keynesian liquidity-preference theory which postulates that the initial, and immediate, effect of monetary growth will be to lower interest rates. What is being questioned is whether the negative relation between money and interest will persist and whether an increase in the money supply is a good prescription for achieving permanently lower interest rates. The evidence from many countries seems to suggest that *tight* money generates *easy* credit and *low* interest rates, and vice versa.4

To see this more clearly, let us suppose a country started increasing the money stock at a rapid rate. If inflations of 15%, 20%, 30%, or higher, get underway, the people who lend money will ask, and receive, interest rates of 35% and 40%, and more. With substantial inflation, everybody knows that the best way to protect a portfolio is to borrow funds and acquire real assets. In consequence, the demand for credit begins rising much faster than the increase in money, and this results in very tight credit. And since debt provides an important means for inflation protection, it should not be surprising that easy money will lead to tight credit.5

The *mutatis-mutandis* association between money and interest rates may at first seem a little bit surprising. The idea that easy money should lead to tight credit is not really surprising, however, when the effects of inflation on the demand for credit are taken into account. From the *mutatis-mutandis* point of view, if the policy goal is to have low interest rates, one must adopt a reasonably good monetary policy, a policy which requires careful control of the money stock.6

Real and Monetary Determinants of Interest Rates

I have questioned the view that easy money will bring about low interest rates; and, instead, have turned this proposition around to suggest that tight money will bring about low interest rates. The question I raise now is this: Are not both of these positions wrong in suggesting that interest rates are determined by the quantity of money?

Let us consider more carefully the factors that determine interest rates. While our discussion seems to suggest that interest rates may be affected by the printing process, it is difficult to accept the proposition that the quantity of money determines interest rates. The interest rate must have something to do with the productivity of capital in relation to the resources made available through saving; and economic theory does suggest that the interest rate does not depend on monetary factors but rather on the productivity of capital and time preference. How can this approach be reconciled with the preceding discussion?

Those analysts who relate interest rates to the theory of capital must surely be right. If interest rates can be reduced either by printing or by destroying money, then it would be very easy to help develop the rest of the world. All we would need are machines that either print or destroy money. If easy money does generate low interest rates, the under-developed countries need printing presses; if tight money leads to lower rates, then these countries need machines that destroy money. Clearly, those who say that interest rates have little to do with money must be right in some sense. All of us who teach macroeconomics and associate money and interest rates need to rationalize this view with the theory of capital, which seems to suggest that interest is not a monetary phenomenon.

Real Interest Rates and Nominal Market Rates

The solution to this dilemma centers on the need to clarify the interest rates that are being considered. If we are concerned with the *real* rate of interest; that is, the rate of return on capital, then the printing of money (Federal Reserve policy) cannot be an effective factor. But the monetary authorities may be able in particular circumstances to affect the market rate of interest.

Interest rates on high-grade corporate bonds—the nominal yields—averaged something like 8% in 1971. Earlier in 1970, it almost reached 10%. In 1946, it fell to an all-time low of 2.1%; in 1965, it was 4½%. These are market rates of interest; they are the yields reported for high-grade (Aaa) corporates in the *New York Times* or the *Wall Street Journal*. The real rate of interest (the rate of return on capital) cannot be observed directly and is not reported in the *New York Times*.

Under what conditions may we infer the movements in the real rates by analyzing market rate developments? One reasonable approach would be to estimate real rates by analyzing the behavior of market rates over a period of fifty to one-hundred years of price stability. Thus, suppose we could obtain interest rate data from a period where everybody was absolutely convinced that the value of money is stable. It seems reasonable to suppose that market rates of interest will tend, in these conditions, to approximate the real rate of interest.7

Today, an individual who buys or sells a bond, or who borrows or lends money, must necessarily involve himself in two different transactions. One is the pure interest rate for the loan of money; the second is the insurance premium that is necessary to protect against fluctuations in the value of money. When market interest rates exceeded 9% in 1970, the insurance premium part of the rate was, perhaps, 4% to 5%. The real interest rate may have been only 4%. Lenders were worried about what was happening to the value of money and thought prices could be rising by 5% a year, and therefore wanted that much of an insurance premium.

Conversely, if everybody knew that prices were expected to decline by 3% a year, it would not be surprising to find market interest rates of approximately 2%. At 2%, a loan of $100 would return $102; but if prices fall 3% over the loan period, the effective loan rate is 5% in real terms. Since $97 this year buys what $100 bought last year, the $102 being returned on the $100 loan implies a real rate of 5% and a nominal rate of 2%.

The market interest rate that changes over time is not necessarily the real rate of interest; it is the money rate of interest. And substantial fluctuations in the money rate take place when people change their views on what is going to be happening to the value of money. As price-level expectations change, so do market rates.

This review of real and nominal rates suggests that market interest rates would tend to approximate the real rate, if the value of money is reasonably stable and if people are not worried about inflation. It also suggests that most of the substantial market interest rate changes reflect fears over the value of money and the associated changes in the insurance premiums, and may have little to do with changes in real rates.

This distinction between market and real rates needs to be emphasized, especially since many people draw important policy conclusions from interest rate movements. Some may infer that the real rate of interest, and therefore the economy, are very volatile because market rates are bouncing around. As a consequence, they may conclude that it is very important for policy-makers in Washington to keep the economy on a straight course. On the other hand, if market interest rates are changing in response to changes in the insurance premium, then it is the effects of inflationary policies that are being observed in the market rate fluctuations. The real rate of interest and the economy may therefore be fairly stable. Policy-makers do not have to develop policies to stabilize the real rates.

Real rates of interest depend on production functions, technology, knowledge, time preference, etc. Nobody really believes that when the Federal Open Market Committee (FOMC) meets every three weeks, and takes a vote, they are affecting the marginal productivity of capital. What the FOMC can affect is the money rate of interest; and the money rate has to be thought of as the real rate of interest (the return on capital) plus the insurance premium.

Consequently, when the money rate bounces around a lot, it does not necessarily mean that the real rate is moving. It could be moving because of changes in the insurance premium. We do not know any general way by which the real rate of interest can be affected. For to do so is to make nature more, or less, productive. Someone can work out an innovation or new productive technique that makes land, or capital, more productive. But such changes in the real rates of return on capital cannot be decided by the FOMC at its meetings.

FOMC and the New Directive: The Monetary Aggregates and Money Market Conditions

The Federal Open Market Committee (FOMC) in 1970 adopted a new directive, changing the operating decisions of monetary policy from a money market strategy to a monetary growth target. Until 1970, both FOMC policies and directives were articulated in terms of money market conditions. Since then, policy has been stated in terms of monetary aggregates. Formerly, when the FOMC met, it formulated a directive giving the account manager instructions to keep the money market in some specified condition, subject to a proviso clause that bank credit or the monetary aggregates do this or that. Under the new directive, the manager is told to keep the monetary aggregates and bank credit growing at certain rates subject to a proviso clause that the money market is not disturbed. The change in wording may not seem significant, but it constitutes a complete turnabout in operating strategy.

Though its primary objective is no longer to stabilize rates, the long-range effect of the change in directive may well be to produce more stable market interest rates. An attempt to stabilize interest rates may destabilize the economy and lead to even greater instability of interest rates. The reason for this situation is that even a small error, when following an interest rate policy, may easily become an open-ended mistake.

Suppose we are seeking to stabilize interest rates, with a goal of a 5% Treasury bill rate. Suppose, however, that a stable economy at the present time requires a 5½% rate. The manager is not able to achieve a 5% rate, but he may explain his failure to hit the target because he is not putting in enough money. As the manager attempts to hit the target by putting in more money, the situation gets more and more out of his control. This is an example of an open-ended error. The example is not really that hypothetical. It describes much of what was happening from 1965 to 1968. The policy-makers came up with the best interest rate estimates they could obtain. If the estimates were even slightly inaccurate, they were in a situation where their errors could easily become larger and larger. That is one great disadvantage of attempting to stabilize interest rates: a small error can easily become a large error that compounds itself.

In contrast, a money stock target provides a self-limiting error mechanism. Errors are, so to speak, self-correcting. Suppose the appropriate money policy is a 4% growth rate, while the operating directive is for 5%. The error will produce inflation of 1%, but it will not feed on itself or lead to higher rates of monetary expansion as an interest rate error will. Moreover, some incentive for an error-reducing correction may develop, insofar as inflation calls for slower monetary growth. It minimizes the likelihood of the big mistakes that are possible with a directive which seeks to stabilize interest rates. The attempt to stabilize rates tends to destabilize the economy and interest rates, whereas an alternative target that does not attempt to stabilize interest rates may indirectly achieve greater stability.

If the Federal Reserve continues this new directive, the results of stabler rates will be apparent in the foreseeable future. The monetary authorities are expected to place greater emphasis on the aggregates because it is now recognized that an interest rate target may be a treacherous vehicle in which to operate policy.

One final point is worth considering briefly. The discussion of real and nominal interest rates in the preceding section seemed to assume that the real rate was determined by nature, and that not much could be done about it through policy. This assumption is not crucial to my argument. One may believe that the real rate of interest can be changed by policy. That is all right. Whether the real rate is relatively fixed, or whether there is some scope for change by policy, will not affect our argument. We assumed a real rate that was relatively fixed to simplify the exposition, but we do recognize that there are circumstances and conditions in which policy can affect the real rate. No one really believes that the real rate of interest went up from 4.5% in 1965 to 10% in 1970. The interest rate escalation since 1965 does not reflect a change in the real rate as much as it does a rise in the insurance premium on the value of money.

Interest Rates as a Temperature Chart

We are now in a better position to understand why a graph of interest rates looks like a fever chart. Suppose that the real rate of interest is relatively stable and that substantive market rate fluctuations reflect the collective doubts about the future value of money. Clearly, when such doubts about the price level become widespread, a country is in trouble. Moreover, no country will, as a deliberate act of policy, "foul up" its finances and risk generating fears that the value of its currency is being eroded. The "foul-ups" usually occur when a country is under pressure, when it is in trouble. The fluctuations in interest rates reflect the public's recognition of the dilemma in governmental finances and the public's uncertainty about inflation and its effects on the value of money. That is why the interest rate chart is, in effect, a fever chart.

If money rates fluctuate primarily because of the public's fears about inflation (deflation), it would follow that the *best* way to reduce market interest rates is to eliminate the insurance premium. This would require that we achieve a climate of opinion in which everybody was absolutely convinced that the value of money would be stable. "Best," in this context, is determined by the price level behavior that is possible, or feasible, under the circumstances.

Better yet may be a world in which commodity prices would decline with increases in productivity, say at a rate of 2% a year. The money rate of interest would then be below the real rate, and it might settle down at 1% or 2%. Unfortunately, most people think that it is Utopian to talk about commodity prices falling with productivity, and one may almost endanger a career by considering such an objective. So, let us forget that I mentioned this possibility and discuss stable prices, a more respectable objective. If stable prices were to prevail, the insurance premium changes would tend to disappear. The money rate of interest would come to reflect the real rate and would, under these circumstances, be fairly stable.

The fifty-year period, in 19th-century England, when the long-term rate was hovering around 3%, hardly fluctuating, provides some evidence on this point. Although that era was one of the calmer periods in recent history, we do not know that it is the real rate of interest we are observing. Large interest rate movements occur when a country is involved in war, or other crises. The racial crisis and the social fragmentation that have occurred in recent years constitute, in this respect, a major problem like a war.

If a country wishes to have low interest rates, it must be able to achieve reasonably good control over money. Stable prices are an efficient way to get low market interest rates; i.e., low nominal rates of interest. I do not consider inflation to be helpful for the developed, or the less developed, countries, for it is difficult to see how inflation *per se* is a source of wealth or of income. I don't think inflation creates jobs. I do think it creates confusion.

Inflation may, for a time, generate a feeling of euphoria, and people may come to believe it generates wealth. In this respect, inflation is like one of the happy pills which provides instant joy. But it is the day after, and the day after that, about which you have to worry. The long-range effects are the important ones. Similarly, I question whether inflation will facilitate development, though some experts would disagree very strongly on this point. In my judgment, however, stable prices are far more desirable.

One of the greatest periods of capital accumulation, expansion, and growth in the United States occurred in the second half of the 19th century—a period of declining commodity prices. This is, therefore, an interesting historical experience to consider. From the Civil War to 1896, commodity prices were declining, and this decline over three decades led to the "cross of gold" speech. However, that era was not a "bad" one in terms of productivity, economic growth, or development. If we had a comparable period again, we would again see great advances. It is not clear how the idea that inflation is good for economic growth developed. Indeed, there is quite a bit of evidence that inflation is not good for growth. Unfortunately, the opposite view has become widespread, and many people think that inflation helps generate greater accumulation, productivity, wealth, economic growth and development.

REFERENCES

1. The recession starting in November 1969, the economic slowdown, and unemployment reaching 6% in 1971, undoubtedly modified some of these attitudes.

2. See D. I. Fand, "Money, Interest and Prices," in *Savings and Residential Financing 1970 Conference Proceedings* (Chicago, 1971.)

3. See D. I. Fand, "Keynesian Monetary Theories, Stabilization, Policy and the Recent Inflation," *Journal of Money, Credit and Banking,* August, 1969.

4. See D. I. Fand, "A Monetarist Model of the Monetary Process," *Journal of Finance,* May 1970, and "Monetarism and Fiscalism," *Banca Nazionale del Lavoro Quarterly Review,* September 1970.

5. See D. I. Fand, "A Monetary Interpretation of the Post-1965 Inflation in the U.S.," *Banca Nazionale del Lavoro Quarterly Review,* June 1969.

6. D. I. Fand, "Some Issues in Monetary Economics," *Banca Nazionale del Lavoro Quarterly Review,* September 1969, and in *Review,* Federal Reserve Bank of St. Louis, January 1970.

7. D. I. Fand, "The 1969-1970 Economic Slowdown," in *Financial Analysts Journal,* January-February 1971.

14

PRELIMINARY NOTES ON THE
SAMARITAN'S DILEMMA

JAMES M. BUCHANAN

I appreciate the opportunity to be able to talk about a topic which commands a good deal of my current interest. I call this "the Samaritan's dilemma."

I am acquainted with an alumnus of a large Ivy League university which has had more than its share of campus turmoil. This acquaintance has had a highly successful business career and has not yet fully disposed of his fortune. He has set up a foundation and has made major gifts to this university over the last two decades. He has been deeply disturbed, however, over the incidents which occurred from 1968 to 1970 at the university. He is very vocal in his condemnation of the university faculty and administration for their failure to react more vigorously against the disruption. Despite his displeasure, however, he is unwilling to withdraw or even to reduce substantially his financial support to the university.

My second example involves a major western university. A clear majority of the governing Board of this university was extremely unhappy with the behavior of the faculty and administrative officials at the university during the campus turmoils of 1968, 1969, and 1970. Despite this, the majority of the regents was totally unwilling to remove university administrators from office, a step clearly within their power.

These two examples from my own experience, represent phenomena which I think pervade not only our society, but all of western culture at this stage in history. This class of phenomena is worth discussing and analyzing in very general terms. Unless its implications are recognized, there may be little hope for anything

15

more than a continuing deterioration of the whole institutional fabric of our society.

I propose to employ the techniques of elementary game theory to present the case and to analyze some of its implications. My central hypothesis is, that modern man has become incapable of making the choices that would be required to prevent his exploitation by predators of his own species. This weakness is imbedded in his own utility functions. It seems appropriate to use the term "dilemma" because the problem is not one which reflects irrational behavior in any of the standard interpretations of rationality.

The causes of this dilemma are in part economic, in that although they do not stem directly from the increasing affluence of choice makers, the analysis does lend some substance to the cliche that modern man has indeed "gone soft" in the sense that his income and utility function now allow options that were not previously observable. If this hypothesis is accepted, the direction of reform and improvement must lie, first of all, in recognizing the dilemma that we are caught in, and secondly, in behaving strategically rather than pragmatically. In other words, the implication is that a person should act in a manner which influences his interacting cohorts to behave in specific ways. The strategy used may require certain behavior patterns that will appear counter to those normally leading to utility maximization when considered independently.

In a wider sense, the analysis lends strong support to the adoption of individual rules for personal choice behavior, as opposed to individual flexibility of action under changing conditions. The concept of individual responsibility is initially derived from strictly individualistic considerations and in an individualistic choice setting, but eventually social or group considerations will emerge. In addition, we can extend the analysis to situations in which individual choices are interdependent, allowing us to convert individual responsibility into social or group responsibility.

I want first to discuss the rules of behavior in personal terms, and then to bring in social or group concepts in the latter part of the discussion.

As mentioned earlier, a highly simplified two-person non-constant-sum game is suggested here as given in Figure 1. The players are the "samaritan" and the "parasite." The samaritan faces two courses of action. He can contribute to the support of the parasite, or he can refuse to contribute. To make the example clear, "contributing" means that he pay $30 a month out of his income to support the parasite. The parasite also has two possible courses of action. Either he works or he does not work. Therefore, there are four possible results, indicated by the Roman numerals in the cells in the matrix.

Figure 1. *The Samaritan's Dilemma*

	The Parasite	
	Work (Column 1)	Not work (Column 2)
Not to contribute to support of the Parasite The Samaritan (Row 1)	I 3,2	II 1,1
Contribute (Row 2)	III 4, 3	IV 2,4

To make our illustration a little more real, we assume that if the parasite does work he can earn an income one-fourth as large as the samaritan's income. The pay-off numbers in the cells of the matrix are simply ordinal indicators representing the levels of utility for the two people. The left-hand number in each cell represents the pay-off to the samaritan, the one on the right represents the pay-off to the parasite. The numbers go from one to four, with four being the most preferred position. The matrix is so constructed that contributing becomes the dominating course of action for the samaritan. "Dominating" simply means that regardless of what the parasite is going to do, the samaritan will find it to his advantage to contribute, because four is larger than three, and two is larger than one. The parasite does not face that sort of dominance, because his choice depends upon what the samaritan is going to do. If the samaritan is expected to contribute, obviously the preferred position to the parasite is not to work. On the other hand, if the samaritan should not contribute, the parasite's preferred choice is to work. The parasite can recognize the dominance in the choices of the samaritan, and the predictable outcome of this game is, of course, that the samaritan will contribute and the parasite will fail to work. Cell IV will be the solution to this particular game.

Obviously, the pay-offs could be arranged to produce a different set of outcomes. But, it can be argued that the above example is an accurate description of behavioral patterns in the real world.

Perhaps the easiest of the rankings to explain for both the samaritan and the parasite are the ones in cell II. It seems likely that they will both assign the lowest rank to this cell because the samaritan surely is not in the habit of sitting by and watching the parasite starve to death, and unless the parasite is suicidal, he will not want to starve to death.

The highest pay-off to the parasite, without much question, is in cell IV. Here he can secure income without working, assuming that to him, work is an inferior activity to receiving charity. Since presumably he does enjoy income, his pay-off in cell III is higher than that in cell I, which in turn is higher than that in cell II.

The samaritan would rather contribute and see the parasite work a bit, therefore his highest pay-off is four in cell III. The next best situation for the samaritan is not to contribute and watch the man work as indicated by pay-off three in cell I. For the samaritan to contribute and watch the man loaf, the pay-off is low (at two) in cell IV. The samaritan's pay-offs of three and two in cells I and IV can be interchanged without really changing the problem.

If the game is played only once, the samaritan would contribute and the parasite would not work. The solution of the game is cell IV. Both the samaritan and the parasite would be maximizing their utilities and there would be no problem. This case would hardly be an interesting dilemma. However, if the game is played continuously, the samaritan would eventually recognize that in the long run he would be better off if he could somehow change the behavior of the parasite.

If the numbers in the cells are taken as cardinal pay-offs, cell III might be considered the "socially preferred situation" because the sum of the two numbers in that cell at seven is the highest for all the cells. The "national product," so to speak, is the greatest in cell III, which is the most efficient position for the two people. To come to the position of cell III, it may be necessary for the samaritan to require the parasite to work as a condition of his contribution. By doing this cell IV is closed out. This strategy may be very difficult for the samaritan to carry out. If the potential parasite behaves strategically, knowing the real pay-off matrix that the samaritan confronts, he may refuse to work and starve. In that case, the samaritan must be willing to cut off the contributions and to watch the parasite starve for a while.

It becomes clear from this example that there is a strong advantage to the samaritan in locking himself into a rule of behavior. As Thomas C. Schelling has explained in his book, *The Strategy of Conflict,* (Cambridge, Harvard University Press, 1960) there are situations where gains are unavailable to a person unless he has locked himself into an irrevocable commitment and the opponent knows this. Over time, the samaritan's utility will be higher if he locks himself into a strategic rule of behavior than it would be if he made particular choice responses to particular choice situations.

In a sense, this pre-selection of a rule for behavior is related to the recognition by the samaritan that utility tomorrow depends upon behavior today. But the dilemma goes a bit beyond that. If it were simply that behavior in future periods is affected by what you do now, then you could simply reduce the problem to the present value of future utility pay-offs and say that the dilemma vanishes. However, the problem of failure to discount the future correctly remains.

An advantage of a pre-selected rule of behavior in advance of a stress situation is that the samaritan need not face the dilemma in its darkest form. For instance, a mother may find it too painful to spank her child and she may let him go without punishment even though she recognizes that if she spanked him today, he would behave better tomorrow, and her utility over time would be increased. In this case, the implication is that she should turn the child over to a nanny or a nurse with specific instructions that he is to be spanked when he misbehaves.

A part of this problem that I have not yet worked out fully is the "natural limits of the discounting process." As noted, people do foresee the effects of current behavior on the utility in the future, but find themselves in this dilemma because they have too high a discount rate with respect to future behavior interactions.

Therefore the question is, can there be a limit on one's discount rate of the future?

For instance, an individual may have a very high discount rate and want to convert all his current capital into income. He can sell all his non-human assets and live it up, and he can borrow against his future income to the limit. He can then sell himself into slavery. That is as far as he can go, a natural limit. But regarding the kind of dilemma discussed here, there is no such simple natural limit.

As suggested, once a person adopts a rule, he should not be responsive to the particulars of a choice situation. This argument specifically refutes the rationality of what is sometimes called "situation ethics." For example, the standards for determining welfare eligibility should not be set by social workers, who directly and personally involve themselves with potential recipients. Social workers are the ones most likely to face the samaritan's dilemma. As another example, university administrators should not enter into the direct dialogues with "concerned" students who are disrupting orderly educational processes. In entering into dialogues, administrators invite the dilemma, while detached adherence to pre-selected rules would avoid it. It seems evident that the student militants recognize this when they complain about the breakdown in communications between themselves and university officials.

To this point the game has been discussed as an isolated event. In reality, games of similar nature may appear in a sequence with only the players changed each time. Each of the players would be confronted with a single play situation, but the behavior of all the players might be treated as if they are involved in a sequential game, because the behavior of any one player might affect the situation facing other players in the future periods. This is very clear in kidnapping and hijacking cases. A pilot may face a hijacker only once and his dominant course of action may be to yield to the hijacker. But what he does is affecting, of course, the possibilities of future hijacking for all other pilots. The same is true of the kidnapping of diplomats. For each of the whole group of players who might face such choices, we find this dilemma re-emerging.

Now let us go back to the situation of my rich alumnus of the Ivy League university. If the alumnus is thinking of making a gift only once and the options are in Figure 2, he simply contributes and is not worried about changing behavior in the future.

More importantly, if he considers his own influence on policies to be negligible, or if he is only one of a thousand, then by changing his behavior he cannot close out any options. This is the standard pub-

Figure 2. *Alumnus' Dilemma*

	Order (Column 1)	Disruption (Column 2)
Not to Contribute (Row 1)	I 3,2	II 1,1
Contribute (Row 2)	III 4,3	IV 2,4

Alumnus

lic goods problem. If there were a thousand alumni in such a situation, obviously the answer is to agree on changes in behavioral standards which would apply to everybody. If we could persuade individuals to adopt rules for behavior that are in the "group" or "social" interest, they might influence the university. The group could get together and agree to form an organization to carry out collective actions. This type of action is discussed at some length in the book, *The Calculus of Consent,* which I wrote with Gordon Tullock, (Ann Arbor, University of Michigan Press, 1962).

If the samaritan group cannot organize itself, individual members might welcome an imposition of rules from outside, if there existed an authority that could impose such rules. Separate university units of a state-wide system might welcome the imposition of a set of uniform rules by the state for dealing with militant students. An individual airline company might welcome federal standards about hijacking. I do not think anyone could doubt that the choice behavior of university administrators on one campus does have a big spill-over effect on the situations faced by administrators on other campuses. It should be recognized that to the extent that people do try to resolve their own personal dilemma by behaving strategically, they also affect the group. There are spill-overs in both directions. Individual responsibility, in the context that I am using it, makes the adherence to a group rule less necessary. Conversely, collective adoption of group rules will make individual response to strategic behavior less necessary. Individual responsibility and group rules are substitutes for each other. The worst of all possible worlds is the one in which neither individual rules of conduct nor voluntary or enforced adherence to jointly selected codes of behavior are enforced and observed. Unfortunately, that seems to be the direction in which modern society is moving.

Increasing economic affluence is one of the reasons why men find themselves in the samaritan's dilemma in twentieth century society. In an impoverished society choices are limited, and people cannot afford soft options. There are very few parasites in a society of paupers. Mothers in a very poor society cannot afford candy to bribe misbehaving children. In a very poor country, students cannot be allowed to live off society until maturity.

The economic explanation, however, may be dwarfed in significance by other historical explanations. The influence of organized religion in earlier periods was surely that of inhibiting behavior that was aimed solely at individual short-run utility maximization. There is valuable content in the Puritan ethic, which, interpreted favorably, resembles what I might call the ethic of group responsibility from a long-run viewpoint. Some of you may be familiar with Professor Edward Banfield's book, *The Unheavenly City*, (Boston, Little Brown, 1970). Professor Banfield argues that one of the major problems of the city is the behavioral attitudes of the lower classes. His definition of "lower classes" is simply that they have a very high discount rate of the future, as opposed to the middle class which is characterized by its emphasis on the future. In this context, I am suggesting that more and more individuals are moving into what Banfield would classify as a lower class attitude.

There might be some ground for guarded and limited optimism if we were to observe the government laying down rules for behavior in situations where individual norms have apparently failed. But what we see is just the opposite. The explanation is that in governments there are instruments promoting the soft options. Governments seem to be loosening up on prescribed rules for behavior, and in this way they encourage short-run utility maximizing behavior on the part of individuals. This pattern of response is, of course, expected, as governments essentially tend to reflect the current desires of the people.

The phenomenon that I have tried to analyze here takes on its most frightening aspects in a very general biological setting. A species that increasingly behaves in a manner which encourages some of its own members to live parasitically off its producing members is self-destructing at some point. Unless an equilibrium is established which imposes some self-selected limits on samaritan behavior, the rush toward destruction may accelerate rather than diminish.

Let us go back to Figure 1. The parasite finds that he does not have to work and the samaritan continues to contribute to his support. Obviously his next move is to force the samaritan to contribute more. The behavior pattern of the samaritan is shifted further away from the most preferred position in cell III. Confronted with the threats of a potential bully, the coward faces a dilemma that is identical to the samaritan's dilemma. The short run utility maximization on the part of the coward suggests surrender, despite its long-run implications. In many real cases, those faced with hard choices are both samaritans and cowards. Who can really tell whether the appeasing university administrator or the faculty member is a samaritan or a coward? It seems to me that some of our student militants have both parasitic and bullyish qualities. At some point the exploitation of the samaritan or the coward must reach a limit, if the species is to survive. The danger is that the limit which is defined by the existing utility functions of modern man may lie beyond that limit which is required to maintain viability in a social order.

SOME ASPECTS OF INTERNATIONAL INFLATION

GARDNER ACKLEY

During the year 1970, prices rose rapidly in the twenty-one member countries of the Organization for Economic Cooperation and Development (OECD). (These countries include essentially all of non-Communist Europe, together with Canada, the United States, and Japan. We will often refer to these countries—somewhat inaccurately— as the "Atlantic Community".) On the average, prices paid by consumers in these countries (the United Kingdom, Japan, Denmark, Sweden, Norway, Spain, Turkey, Iceland, and Ireland) the year's increase in consumer prices was 7 per cent or more. In only six countries (Germany, Canada, Belgium, Greece, Portugal, and Finland) was the consumer price rise 4½ per cent or less.[1] Moreover, the advance of prices was only moderately faster during 1970 than in a number of other recent years. No wonder that some have referred to the present as an "age of inflation."

Meaning and measurement of inflation

Although in the past the term has sometimes been given other meanings, today there is general agreement that inflation is best defined simply as "a persistent rise in the general level of prices of goods and services." "Persistent" means more than temporary— lasting over a span of several years—and many connote a price rise which in some sense "feeds on itself." A rise in the "general level of

---

This lecture was expanded and published under the title, *Stemming World Inflation* by the Atlantic Institute, (Paris, 1971). Permission has been obtained from the author and the publisher for reprinting the lecture portion here.

[1] The data compare consumer prices in the 4th quarter of 1970 with the 4th quarter of 1969.

24

prices" does not mean that every single price rises, nor that all prices rise by the same amount, but only that individual price increases, taking into account both their amount and the importance of the goods and services in which they occur, outweigh price declines.[1]

Movements of the general price level are measured by a "price index number."[2] The price indexes of broadest coverage are those called "gross national product (GNP) deflators" or, because of the method of their calculation, "implicit price indexes of GNP," or simply "implicit deflators." These indexes, which are available (and with some delay) mainly for the larger countries, attempt to measure the average price movement of all goods and services included in GNP: that is, all "final" goods and services produced in an economy. ("Final" goods consist of finished consumer goods and services at retail; new capital goods—currently produced buildings, machines, etc.; goods and services sold to governments; and exports minus imports.) The price index of more limited coverage which is most used and most useful is that for consumer goods and services alone, sometimes—inaccurately—called a "cost-of-living" index. Such indexes are rather promptly available for every country of the Atlantic Community (although not necessarily of equal quality). Their availability leads to their frequent use in international comparisons; unfortunately, especially for this purpose, they are inferior to GNP deflators. The indexes of "wholesale prices" prepared in many countries summarize the movements of prices for a wide variety of *goods* (usually excluding all or most *services*) when sold other than at retail.

Price indexes (often of consumer prices) are used to correct or "deflate" data on money or "nominal" incomes. The resulting "deflated" data are said to measure "real incomes"—that is, incomes expressed in terms of the aggregate quantity of real goods

---

[1] If direct controls prevent what would otherwise have been a persistent rise in prices, many prefer to say that inflation nevertheless exists: "suppressed inflation."

[2] To compute this number, the price of each of a large number of representative individual goods and services in each month, quarter, or year is first expressed as a percentage of what it had been in some more recent year (taken as "base period"). Each such percentage is given a "weight" proportional to the money value of the output which it represents. All of these weighted percentages, for each month year, or quarter, are then averaged into a single "index number," which thus indicates the weighted average percentage which prices in the particular period are of those in the base period. Such price indexes generally exclude the prices of "productive services"—that is, wage rates of workers, interest rates on loans, profit rates of business—and exclude, as well, the prices of assets—e.g., shares or bonds, existing buildings, land, antique furniture and paintings, etc. (Indexes of wage rates, interest rates, share prices, land prices, etc., are sometimes computed, and have their purposes; but they are not usually considered as direct indicators of inflation.)

and services they will buy. Measures of the money value of output, when deflated, are referred to as measures of "real output"—that is, they show changes in the "physical volume" of production.

Because of defects of concept or coverage—some of which are, even in principle, unavoidable—the accuracy of any price index is less than perfect, even in those countries which devote the most money and care to their preparation. Measures of real income and real output are similarly impaired. In particular, it is generally agreed that almost all price indexes have a built-in tendency to exaggerate the extent to which prices are increasing. Without going into detail, this "upward bias" arises in part from our ability fully to measure improvements in the "quality" of goods sold (an improved quality, sold at the same price, just like a larger quantity sold at the same price, is really a price reduction).[1] Much more important is our ability to measure the improvement in the "quality" of the whole assortment of goods and services available on the market, which arises from the introduction of completely new goods and services, previously unavailable. Whether this bias is of the order of ¼ of 1 per cent a year, or as much as 1½ or 2 per cent a year is a matter of debate among economists.

For this reason, as well as because a small upward creep in prices (as measure) is both extremely difficult to avoid and probably not seriously harmful, some authorities reserve the term inflation for a persistent rise exceeding (say) 1 or 2 per cent a year in the conventional price indexes. Other economists reach a similar judgement, but framed in a rather different way. However they may choose to define inflation, they prefer to emphasize the particular importance of industrial prices—that is, of the price level excluding food and services. They regard the stability of industrial prices as representing a fully satisfactory achievement. In most countries, stability of industrial prices would be consistent with a rise of from 1 to 2 or even 2½ per cent a year in the consumer price index or GNP deflator.

The extent of inflation, 1955-70

Even such minimal rates of price increase (2 or 2½ per cent a year) have been exceeded most of the time in recent years in every country of the Atlantic Community. Table 1 (see page 27) shows the average annual change and the cumulative change in the

---

[1] Not all quality changes are improvements, of course. Sometimes, especially during periods of inflation, deliberate quality deterioration is a hidden form of price increase.

GNP deflator in each of the principal Atlantic countries over the past fifteen years, along with average changes for these countries as a group. Table 2 (see page 28) shows changes in the consumer price index of the 22 counties over the same period. The tables show that the average annual price increase in the Atlantic Community has been a little more than 3 per cent over these 15 years.

Among the larger countries, only Italy, during 1955-60, and the United States and Canada, during 1960-65, had half-decade inflation rates as low as 2 per cent, as measured by GNP deflators. Germany, Canada, and Japan also met this standard during 1955-60, measured in terms of consumer prices. Among the smaller countries, Belgium, Switzerland, Denmark, and Luxembourg, during 1955-60, and Greece during 1960-65, experienced inflation of 2 per cent or less for a half decade, as measured by the change in consumer prices. No country met this standard during 1965-70, either in terms of GNP deflators or consumer prices.

Table 1

Price Changes in Major Countries, 1955-70
as Measured by GNP Deflators

| | Average annual percentage increase | | | | Cumulative percentage increase |
	1955-60	1960-65	1965-70	1955-70	1955-70
Germany	2.7	3.6	3.4	3.2	61
France	6.5	4.1	4.6	5.0	109
Italy	2.0	5.5	3.4	3.6	70
United Kingdom	3.2	3.4	4.7	3.8	74
Canada	2.6	1.9	4.1	2.9	53
United States	2.6	1.5	4.0	2.7	48
Japan	3.3	5.0	4.7	4.3	88
Average, seven countries*	3.0	2.6	4.1	3.2	61

*Weighted by 1969 GNP

Source: Publications of the OECD and national authorities. Deflators for 1970 are partially estimated.

Table 2

Price Changes In Countries of the Atlantic Community 1955-70, as Measured by Consumer Price Indexes

	Average annual percentage increase				Cumulative percentage increase
	1955-60	1960-65	1965-70	1955-70	1955-70
Germany	1.8	2.8	2.6	2.4	43
France	5.8	3.8	4.3	4.6	97
Italy	1.9	4.9	2.9	3.2	61
United Kingdom	2.6	3.5	4.6	3.6	69
Canada	1.9	1.6	3.9	2.5	44
United States	2.1	1.3	4.3	2.5	45
Japan	1.5	6.0	5.5	4.3	89
Average, seven major countries*	2.3	2.5	4.2	3.0	56
Netherlands	2.6	3.5	4.9	3.7	73
Belgium	1.7	2.5	3.5	2.6	47
Luxembourg	1.5	2.1	3.0	2.2	39
Norway	2.8	4.1	4.9	3.9	78
Sweden	3.6	3.6	4.4	3.9	78
Denmark	1.7	5.5	6.4	4.6	96
Finland	6.7	4.9	4.7	5.6	126
Austria	2.1	3.9	3.3	3.1	58
Switzerland	1.2	3.2	3.5	2.8	47
Spain	7.8	7.0	5.1	6.7	163
Portugal	2.1	2.6	6.4	3.7	71
Greece	2.3	1.6	2.5	2.1	38
Turkey	14.4	3.7	8.2	8.6	248
Ireland	2.6	4.2	5.3	4.0	81
Iceland	4.6	10.8	12.9	9.4	284
Average, 15 smaller countries*	4.1	4.0	4.7	.34	94
Average, 22 countries*	2.6	2.7	4.3	3.2	61

*Weighted by 1969 GNP

Source: Publications of the OECD and the IMF.

Prices rising at 2 per cent a year, compounded, will produce a rise of nearly 35 per cent over 15 years. No country came close to that during 1955-70. The average cumulative rise during this period for the major countries was 61 per cent as measured by GNP deflators and 56 per cent as measured by consumer prices. For all 22 countries, the average cumulative rise of consumer prices was 61 per cent. The United States, with 45 per cent, Germany, with 43 per cent, and Canada, with 44 per cent, had the best 15-year records among the major countries, along with Belgium, Luxembourg, Switzerland, and Greece among the smaller countries.

A longer-term comparison

Inflation at an average rate of 3 per cent a year, although it could still be characterized as mild, nevertheless contrasts sharply with the movement of price levels between the two world wars. Table 3 (see page 30), taken from a recent OECD study, compares the experience of seven Atlantic countries during the "inter-war" period, 1925-1938, and the "post-war" period, 1955-1965. The difference in price behavior, shown in columns 5 and 6, is striking: in each of the countries, the inter-war period was characterized by price stability or a slightly declining price level; in the post-war period each country's price level was rising. Equally striking, however, are the differences shown in columns 1 and 2, and 3 and 4. These data make abundantly clear that the post-war Atlantic world has been an infinitely more prosperous and economically rewarding one: in each of the countries, economic growth was distinctly faster in the post-war period than during the inter-war period—replacing what in some cases was complete stagnation —and jobs were available for a substantially larger fraction of the working force—replacing in some cases mass unemployment.

There can be little doubt that so revolutionary a change, occurring simultaneously in each of the Atlantic countries shown, and surely in the others as well, was no accident. Something new had happened everywhere in the Atlantic world. No doubt there were many economic, social, and political trends which influenced the result. But, surely, the most crucial thing that had happened was the assumption by each government, at the end of World War II, of a responsibility to promote full employment and economic prosperity. This assumption of responsibility was possible only because of a revolution that had occurred in economic knowledge and understanding. The principal tools of intervention on behalf of prosperity (government spending, taxes, money supply) were not new: only they were used in a new way, and with a new consciousness of their power.

Table 3

Inter-war and Post-war Growth, Unemployment, and Prices

	Average Annual % Change in GNP		Average Level of Unemployment, % of Labour Fource		Average Annual % Change in Consumer Prices	
	Inter-war 1925-38	Post-war 1955-65	Inter-war 1925-38	Post-war 1955-65	Inter-war 1925-38	Post-war 1955-65
	1	2	3	4	5	6
Belgium	0	4	6½	2½	0	2½
France	0	5½	3	1	0	4¾
Germany	4	6	8	2	−1	2¾
Italy	2	6	4½	5	0	3½
Sweden	3	4	5	2	− ½	4
United Kingdom	2½	3	9	1½	−1	3½
United States	1	4	14	5	− ½	1¾

1. For statistical and other reasons, comparisons should not be made between the levels of unemployment in different countries. Minor changes in the level within the same country may only reflect differences in the manner of collecting the statistics.

Source: OECD, Fiscal Policy for a Balanced Economy: Experience, Problems, and Prospects (the Report of a Committee consisting of Walter Heller, Cornelis Goedhart, Guillaume Guindey, Heinz Haller, Jean van Houtte, Assar Lindbeck. Richard Sayers, and Sergio Steve, with the collaboration of J.C.R. Dow), December 1968, p. 80. (Sources of the particular data are shown in the original. Although not so indicated, the GNP data obviously are changes in "real" GNP. The changes shown in consumer prices during 1955-65 are not in all cases fully consistent with data in table 2, but are of similar orders of magnitude.)

But if new government policies are responsible for the vastly superior economic performance, it seems clear that they must also accept some responsibility for the shift from the previous price stability to the inflation—however mild—that has universally risen. To be sure, if the price of the greater prosperity and faster growth was a mild inflation averaging 3 per cent a year, most people would probably agree that this was a price well worth paying. Still, three important sets of questions need to be raised and are increasingly being raised about this proposition:

1. Are we sure that we can continue to enjoy the benefits of the post-war prosperity along with only a mild inflation? Is there not danger that a mild inflation will accelerate? Indeed, is there not evidence that such an acceleration is already under way?

2. What are the true costs of a mild inflation? Could they not be more serious than we think?

3. Was even the mild inflation of 1955-70 a *necessary* price for the economic achievements of our post-war world? With even better policies, could we have enjoyed post-war prosperity along with something closer to pre-war price stability? Is there any prospect that we can do better in the years ahead? How should we go about trying to improve our price performance?

Table 4

Annual and Half-Year Price Changes, 1965-70
in Major Countries, as Measured by GNP Deflators

	Percentage change					Percentage change at annual rates		
	1966 1965	1966 1967	1968 1967	1969 1968	1970 1969	I-1969 II-1969	II-1969 II-1970	I-1970 I-1970
Germany	3.8	0.7	1.9	3.4	7.4	6.6	8.0	7.3
France	2.9	2.7	4.8	7.0	5.6	5.3	6.0	5.0
Italy	2.2	2.8	1.5	4.0	6.3	5.3	6.8	6.0
United Kingdom	4.4	3.1	4.0	5.0	7.3	4.9	7.3	9.0
Canada	4.6	3.7	3.6	4.7	4.1	3.3	5.3	2.4
United States	2.8	3.1	4.1	4.8	5.1	5.3	5.4	4.9
Japan	4.5	4.3	3.4	4.2	6.6	7.3	6.6	6.0
Average, seven countries*	3.2	3.0	3.7	4.8	5.7	5.6	6.0	5.5

*Weighted by 1969 GNP

Source: Publications of the OECD and national authorities. Data for II-1970 and therefore for year 1970 are partly estimated.

Much of the rest of this study is designed to throw light on these questions. The question whether we are already experiencing an acceleration of inflation occupies the remainder of this chapter. The costs of inflation are analyzed in Chapter 2. Chapters 3 and 4 attempt to summarize the causes of inflation in the Atlantic world and Chapter 5 the methods that have been and may be used to control it. This analysis implies at least tentative answers to the third group of questions.

An acceleration of inflation?

Tables 1 and 2 showed that the average rate of price increase during the most recent half decade—1965-70—substantially exceeded that of the two previous 5-year periods. Of the three 5-year periods, the most recent was the most inflationary in three of the major countries and in eleven of the others. It is interesting to note that, on average, the 15 smaller countries experienced a much steadier, although faster, rate of inflation than the major countries, the average rising only from 4.1 per cent during 1955-65 to 4.7 per cent in 1965-70.

Tables 4 and 5 record the year-by-year course of price increases within the last half decade, together with the most recent half-year changes.[1] They show that the average rate of inflation in each of the past five years was higher than the average for the previous decade. Moreover, there was a clear acceleration in the rate of price increase beginning in 1968 for all countries together, and for the major countries taken as a group. The years 1969 and 1970 were years of the fastest inflation the Atlantic Community has known since the period of post-World War II reconstruction and the Korean War. By 1970 the average price increase had reached a rate more than twice the average of 1960-65.

Nevertheless, a pattern of generally accelerating inflation within these five years is not characteristic of most countries individually. In no country was the acceleration of inflation uninterrupted, although it was essentially so for the United States. Outside the major countries, there is almost no suggestion of a trend towards acceleration. In only 10 of the 22 countries was the 1969-70 increase in consumer prices the largest of the five annual changes.

---

[1] Annual movements in consumer prices were influenced in several cases by special factors, including changes in rates or systems of indirect taxation. In this period, this was the case in one or more years for the United Kingdom, the Netherlands, Belgium, Norway, Sweden, and Denmark.

Table 5

Annual and Half-Year Price Changes, 1965-70
as Measured by Consumer Price Indexes

	Percentage change					Percentage change at annual rates		
	1965 1966	1966 1967	1967 1968	1968 1969	1969 1970	I-1969 II-1969	II-1969 I-1970	I-1970 II-1970
Germany	3.5	1.5	1.8	2.7	3.8	1.5	5.9	2.2
France	2.7	2.7	4.6	6.4	5.3	5.2	6.3	5.0
Italy	2.3	3.2	1.4	2.6	5.0	4.4	5.5	4.5
United Kingdom	3.9	2.5	4.7	5.5	6.4	3.2	7.7	6.9
Canada	3.7	3.5	4.2	4.5	3.4	4.9	3.5	1.6
United States	2.9	2.8	4.2	5.4	5.9	6.1	6.1	5.3
Japan	5.1	4.0	5.4	5.2	7.7	7.8	8.0	7.0
Average, seven major countries*	3.2	2.8	4.0	5.0	5.7	5.4	6.2	5.1
Netherlands	5.8	3.4	3.7	7.5	4.4	1.9	5.1	5.8
Belgium	4.2	2.9	2.7	3.8	3.9	3.9	4.5	2.8
Luxembourg	3.3	2.2	2.6	2.3	4.7	2.0	6.7	3.3
Norway	3.3	4.4	3.5	3.1	10.6	3.4	15.6	7.9
Sweden	6.4	4.3	1.9	2.7	7.1	3.5	9.2	6.2
Denmark	6.7	6.9	8.6	4.2	6.7	5.0	6.1	8.8
Finland	3.5	6.0	9.0	2.7	2.7	1.7	3.4	2.6
Austria	2.2	3.9	2.8	3.0	4.4	3.5	4.5	4.9
Switzerland	4.8	3.9	2.5	2.5	3.6	1.8	3.4	5.8
Spain	6.2	6.5	4.9	2.2	5.7	3.2	5.2	9.3
Portugal	5.0	5.5	6.1	8.8	6.4	7.2	6.7	5.0
Greece	5.1	1.6	0.4	2.4	3.2	1.1	4.1	3.5
Turkey	8.7	14.0	5.3	4.8	6.9	4.2	9.6	8.7
Ireland	2.9	3.2	4.7	7.3	8.2	5.8	8.5	10.0
Iceland	11.1	3.2	14.8	2.4	13.0	17.0	10.0	17.2
Average, 15 smaller countries*	5.4	5.0	4.0	3.9	5.4	3.2	6.3	6.3
Average, 22 countries*	3.5	3.1	4.1	5.0	5.8	5.3	6.4	5.3

*Weighted by 1969 GNP

Source: Publications of the OECD and national authorities.

The fact that the United States accounts for roughly half of the total GNP of the 22 countries combined, automatically imprints the U.S. pattern rather heavily on the weighted average for all countries, and in the United States the acceleration of inflation was strong and uninterrupted (except briefly during 1967) for special reasons which one may hope will not be repeated. Moreover, to some extent, the pattern of price increase in other countries has been influenced by that of the United States (through mechanisms that are sketched in Chapter 4).

One hopeful development is that price increases slowed down in the second half of 1970 in a number of countries, particularly the major ones, as is apparent by comparing the last two columns in Tables 4 and 5. However, it appears that this largely reflects seasonal elements in many of the major European countries. The data becoming available for the early months of 1971 suggest that only in the United States, Canada, and France, among the major countries, has inflation clearly slowed down since the first half of 1970. The trend is not yet clear for Japan, Germany, and Italy, and it is clearly towards a continuing acceleration of inflation in the United Kingdom. Among the smaller countries, a genuine slowing-down seems indicated only for Austria and Denmark, while price increases apparently are continuing to accelerate in Norway, Spain, Switzerland, and Iceland.

Because of the great importance of the United States—both directly and through her influence on prices elsewhere—the slowing-down of price increases in that country, while rates of inflation are at least no longer increasing in many others, provides some hope that, for the present at least, the trend will be towards lower rates of inflation in the Atlantic Community. It is important to recognize, however, that this modest improvement has been purchased at the cost of substantial unwanted unemployment in the United States, Canada, and the United Kingdom, and a slowing-down of rates of increase of output in most of the other major countries. Relative to rates of unemployment, inflation remains at an unprecedentedly high rate.

If the United States should succeed in getting her recent inflation firmly under control, and were to resume approximately the degree of price stability she enjoyed prior to 1966, it could be that the Atlantic Community as a whole might expect an inflation no worse than the 2½ to 3 per cent rate that prevailed from 1955 to 1965. Clearly, much depends on what will happen to prices in the United States in the next few years.

There is, however, no possible basis for complacency about the outcome. Even with the recent slowing down in some countries, inflation remains at an uncomfortably high rate almost everywhere. Surely, the experience of the past fifteen years, and the analysis which will be developed in the subsequent chapters of this study, strongly suggest that the problem of inflation may now be rather deeply-rooted in the economic conditions and institutional structures of the Atlantic countries, and will not readily be overcome. There are few who believe that price increases in the United States are likely to return to the negligible rate of the early 1960s (a period when unemployment was substantially in excess of U.S. official targets). Indeed, some fear that, once the U.S. economy again begins to expand more rapidly, as is the express goal of current government policy, the substantial rates of inflation experienced in the late 1960s might well return. In that case, there will be no question that inflation has definitely accelerated, and there will be increased basis for fears of still further acceleration.

A more general theory of inflation

Admitting the possibility that both kinds of inflationary forces can occur calls attention to the "mixed"forms of inflation in which both demand-pull and cost-push forces are present. We can, for example, recognize that an inflationary process may be initiated by forces of demand and sustained by those of cost push, even after the demand forces that initiated the inflation have faded out of existence.[1] Similarly, an inflation which begins with a cost push could strengthen aggregate demand sufficiently to generate some upward "pull" on prices as well. This could happen if the initial "push" redistributed income from groups having a low propensity

---

[1] One version even explains how inflation may arise from a mere *shift* of demand from one sector of industry or class of products to another, with no excess of aggregate demand. The higher demand for the products or services for which demand has increased raises their prices and the incomes earned in their production; but downward rigidity of other prices and wages prevents any off-setting decline in prices in the areas for which demand is reduced. Thus the general level of prices is raised, and organized workers seek extra wage increases to offset the rising cost of living (some may get such increases automatically through "sliding-scale" or escalator provisions). Indeed, workers generally may seek not only protection from the higher cost of living, but to match the real-wage gains secured by those whose wages benefited from the initial raise in demand. The localized wage and price increase is thus generalized, and an inflationary spiral is initiated. Market forces call for what should be a mere rearrangement of relative prices and wages; but rigidities, and the unwillingness of those who would suffer from the rearrangement to accept the relative worsening of their incomes, convert the rearrangement of relative prices into an upward movement of the entire price level. If the subsequent rise in *other* wages and prices prevents the shift of resources into increased production of the goods initially in larger demand, prices may be further bid up in that area, helping to perpetuate the spiral.

to spend in favour of those who would spend much or all of the extra incomes they obtained. Moreover, an initial cost-push rise of prices might generate expectations of further rise, which would cause buyers to step up their spending in an effort to beat the price rise, thus helping to insure continuance of the inflation.

But we have arrived not merely at the recognition of possible "mixtures" of two separate types of inflation. Rather, we have reached a more general analysis of inflation, which can replace the dichotomous approach followed up to this point. This more general analysis incorporates important elements drawn from both demand-pull and cost-push theories, along with other significant considerations included in neither. Some of these other elements have already been referred to, but will be further considered in subsequent paragraphs.

1. *Downward rigidity of wages and prices.* Most wage rates, along with the goods and services, other than farm products and internationally-traded raw materials, are not equally flexible in an upward and downward direction, in response to variations in the strength of aggregate demand. To be sure, there are many industries in which productivity gains are exceedingly rapid, and the trend of whose prices may be downward except during the most inflationary periods. But the reference here is to an asymmetrical response of prices to the strengthening as opposed to the weakening of demand. When demand slackens, firms in many industries resist price declines as long as they possibly can, and prefer to make them, if at all, by giving selective and temporary discounts from standard prices. But when markets strengthen beyond some point, they readily raise their price schedules. Today, outright wage rate reductions rarely if ever occur in most countries. Downward inflexibility arises from minimum wage laws, and from social disapproval of direct action to reduce a worker's pay. Of course, many workers suffer wage reductions when they lose their jobs and can only find another at lower pay. Pay is also frequently reduced by shorter working weeks or the loss of overtime. But these do not reduce basic costs of production as would wage rate reductions.

The asymmetry between the upward and downward flexibilities of wages and price rests on a very simple and fundamental fact. For any individual seller of goods or labour (or of anything else), a reduction of price or wage means a reduction of real income; an increase means an increase of real income. People like higher incomes, dislike lower ones; they seek the one and resist the other. It is true that a reduction of the whole wage-price level has no effect on real incomes—nor a rise, either. But no individual wage or price reduction (or increase) can ever be accurately described as merely part of a general price level change.

Downward inflexibility of wages and prices creates a severe bias towards inflation right from the start. Prices and wages are essentially on a ratchet. They move easily upwards, but rarely and with difficulty downwards. Circumstances that cause an appreciable number of individual prices and wages to rise almost surely cause the average price level to rise: offsets in the form of lower prices and wages are rarely available. Instead, the rise in some prices and wages tends to produce increases in others. This phenomenon of downward price and wage rigidity will be further referred to below.

2. *The pattern of productivity, wage rate, and unit labour cost changes.* Although the advance of productivity over time occurs reasonably smoothly and steadily for whole economies, its advance is likely to be both jerky and unequal in particular sectors, industries, or firms. In the United States, for instance, the advance of productivity has tended for many years to be remarkably rapid in the agricultural sector, considerably in excess of that in any other major sector. Among the non-agricultural sectors, the trend of productivity gains ranges from an average of 5 or 6 per cent a year in public utilities and communications, to 1 or 2 per cent a year in services. Mining, manufacturing, transport, trade, and construction fall between the extremes, in roughly descending order. Somewhat the same ranking holds in other countries, although there are major exceptions. The diversity of productivity trends of course becomes all the wider as we consider finer subdivisions of economic activity —e.g., industries, or even firms, instead of these broad sectors. Within manufacturing, for example, many of the new industries generate rapid productivity gains, while more traditional industries are likely to show gains more like those occurring in the service trades.

What this diverse behaviour of productivity gains implies for the individual trends of unit labour costs, and hence of prices, in the various sectors, industries, and firms that make up the economy depends on what happens to wage rates in different industries and firms. For example, if the average wage rate in each industry should rise in exact proportion to the rise of productivity in that industry, unit labour costs would be constant over time in every industry. Or, if the wage rate in each industry should rise by the increase in productivity in that industry, plus 3 per cent, unit labour costs would rise by 3 per cent in every industry.

This kind of pattern of wage increases is not, however, likely to occur, nor would it, in general, be a desirable outcome if it did. Instead of wages rising in proportion to productivity—industry-by-industry, or even firm-by-firm—there are strong forces tending to impose a considerable uniformity in the movement of wage rates. One reason is that all industries and firms must compete with each other for workers. If the wage rates offered in a single labour market for any particular type and quality of labour differ substantially, those employers who offer the lower wages will have trouble attracting or retaining workers, at least in times of high employment. Moreover, difference in wage rates as among various labour market areas or geographical regions, or among workers of various types, qualities, or skills must bear some relationship to the relative attractiveness of the work and the costs of qualifying for it—at least to the extent that workers are able to change their residence, undertake training, or gain experience that permits them to shift among categories in response to changing differentials.

To be sure, the information which workers receive about the wages paid by various employers, and the associated job requirements, is far from perfect in every national labour market. And workers' mobility as among employers, industries, occupations, and regions in response to whatever information they have as to the opportunities available to them is also far from perfect. This is one reason why expanding firms may need to pay substantially higher wage rates to attract workers from other employments. It also means that wage differentials may emerge and may persist for considerable periods, that would be erased if information and mobility were better. Moreover, one objective of trade unions is to raise wages for their own members, and their unequal effectiveness in doing this tends to create further persistent wage differences, particularly to the extent that the unions are able to control entry into their trade or employment.

Nevertheless, competition does *tend* to make wage rates move more or less together over time, and this tendency is strongly reinforced by concepts of equity or social justice, as well as by the rather powerful forces of imitation and jealousy.

These forces, both competitive and institutional, which cause wages to move more or less similarly over time have several consequences, any one or more of which may be exceedingly important for the inflationary process in a particular economy at a particular time.

a. If some groups of workers receive large wage increases—

because of a sharp rise in the demand for their services, because they have increased their ability to exclude others from entering their trade, or simply because their trade union has become more aggressive or effective in its bargaining—this imposes a strong tendency for wages in other industries and occupations to be similarly raised, generating an extra rise in unit labour costs and hence in prices throughout the economy.

b. The forces imposing a tendency towards wage uniformity make it exceedingly difficult for relative wage rates—and thus the distribution of wage income among various groups or classes of workers—to be altered significantly in the market, however unjust or socially inappropriate existing income differentials are felt to be. Efforts of workers or employers to alter wage differentials in favour of one group of workers will be largely frustrated by the extra wage increases demanded and received by others. Successful action to alter differentials may instead require programmes which will effectively alter relative supplies of labour of various types: through special training programmes, special aids to mobility, or the breaking down of artificial barriers against the entry into various trades and occupations.

c. To the extent that wage-rate changes tend to be similar in all industries, while productivity trends differ widely (as they do), the trends of unit labour costs in various industries will be quite diverse. If the price level is to remain stable, this means not merely that the general rate of wage increases must be close to the average rate of productivity rise, but also that prices must decline in the industries in which productivity rises by more than the average rate. If, for any reason, such price decreases fail to occur, price stability cannot be maintained. In the first place, mere arithmetic requires that price increases in the industries with less than average productivity gains be offset by price reductions in industries with more than average gains. If the reductions fail to occur, the average price level will rise. Moreover, if wages rise only in proportion to productivity, but the average price level nevertheless increases, the resulting shift in the distribution of real income from labour to owners of enterprises will lead workers to demand larger wage increases, which raise the average level of labour costs. Most particularly, the failure to reduce prices in industries with large productivity gains but wage increases proportional only to the economy-wide average productivity increase creates large profit gains in such industries, which become tempting targets for the trade-union wage demands. If extra large increases are secured in such high-profit industries, they will be copied elsewhere, pushing up labour costs and prices across the board.

3. *Further institutional aspects of the inflationary process.* A great many institutional arrangements, which nominally or traditionally exist for other reasons, turn out to play a significant role in the intersectoral transmission and the perpetuation of inflation. For instance, if firms set prices so as to yield some standard percentage mark-up over specified elements of direct costs, and there is much evidence that they do, this tends to convert every rise in wages or material prices into a proportionate rise in selling prices. Yet when the level of costs is constantly changing, firms may have little choice but to follow such a formula. Following a "pattern" set by the most recent wage increase in another firm or industry (or, perhaps, the *highest* among the recent wage increases agreed on in other firms or industries) is an easy way to resolve otherwise irreconcilable claims in bargaining. It is also a way to guarantee that an inflationary spiral will continue to turn. Yet the development and imitation of wage "patterns" can be shown to play a major role in wage bargaining in many countries.

Institutional arrangements relating to the process of wage determination are exceedingly important in the dynamics of inflation. The tradition of contracts for fixed terms—increasingly two- and three-year terms in the United States—provides a great element of inertia: preserving stability once this is achieved, but perpetuating inflation once this is underway. U.S. labour contracts negotiated in 1962-64 provided a built-in stability of labour costs in many industries for several years afterwards. Similarly, wage contracts agreed upon in 1970 have already provided large wage increases for many workers in both 1971 and 1972; large wage increases in 1971 are built into other contracts negotiated in 1969. Workers negotiating new agreements in 1971 will wish to do at least that well.

The stability of labour costs provided by long-term contracts negotiated during non-inflationary periods is at least potentially compromised if those contracts provide escalator clauses, as an increasing number of U.S. agreements do. To be sure, escalator provisions have no impact on wage rates if prices do not rise. But they quickly spread or generalize, and perpetuate, upward movements of prices that originate elsewhere. Wage rates inevitably respond in any case to rising prices, even without formal escalator provisions. But the response is full, prompt, and automatic where escalator provisions exist, whereas in their absence it is likely to be partial, delayed, and to require negotiation. Moreover, there is no clear evidence that the existence of escalator provisions results in the agreement on substantially smaller "basic" wage increases in multi-year contracts negotiated during inflationary periods. And, of course, escalator provisions are never permitted to operate to reduce wage rates. Their use in the United States and probably elsewhere must be judged to strengthen an institutional bias towards inflation.

Where wage agreements are made for an unspecified term, as for example in the United Kingdom, the institutional forces are different. Such agreements can provide little assured stability of labour costs. Whether a new agreement has embodied a large or a small increase can only be determined by how long it lasts before it is again revised. To the extent that current economic conditions affect negotiated wage changes, the British agreement can be more responsive than the U.S. contract: in a less inflationary environment, reopening of the agreement can be delayed; in a more inflationary environment it can be speeded up and the size of the increase also enlarged. Because of this—in the inflationary environment—the British system seems to threaten a "double-whammy": an early reopening that increases the average size of the last increase, and a large new increase to reflect current and expected conditions.

The structure of trade union organization can also be of great importance in explaining wage movements: the extent of centralization of authority in top union officers versus control by the "rank and file"; the existence or not of competitive unions with the same or overlapping jurisdictions; organization by craft versus industry; the power and influence of national union federations; union affiliation with political parties that may be in or out of the government; and many others.

Systems of centralized bargaining—such as those in the Netherlands or Sweden—permit, indeed, almost require, that negotiators be conscious of the effect of their negotiated wage increase on the level of prices. Thus it is easier for those on the labour side to recognize that much or all of what labour might appear to gain from an excessive settlement is illusory. Whatever extra amount workers may gain in higher wages, beyond some point, will be lost through higher prices. The highly decentralized bargaining practiced in the United States, on the other hand, makes the size of any individual settlement essentially irrelevant for the prices the workers will pay. Thus, the interest of the negotiators on the labour side in getting the largest possible increase in money wages is not appreciably compromised by any consideration of its effect on prices.

The belief that what happens to prices is independent of the size of any—and thus of *every*—wage settlement is also nourished by the myth that, since the wage bargain is in the first instance made between a union and an employer, a wage dispute can only be an argument about the division of the "pie" between wages and profits, and not about the division of the "pie" among this group of workers, its employer, and its employer's customers—most of whom are other workers. This myth may be reinforced by economic doctrines which assert that the level of prices depends on competition, or the level of demand, the money supply, or some other outside force. That each group of workers believes or at least perpetuates this myth about the effect of its own bargaining is not strange, for it is obviously so comforting and self-serving a doctrine. What is more difficult to understand is how workers often can appear to believe it with respect to other workers' bargaining—even those much better paid than themselves—and how it can be unquestioningly accepted—at least in the United States—by many highly educated middle-class "liberals" in the professions, government, the universities, and the information media.

If questioned as to who will pay for a large wage increase, an educated and public-spirited U.S. citizen is quite likely to reply that "profits are big enough to absorb it." He will have no conception whatever of how *much* of a reduction in profits would be required for a business to absorb a (say) 10 per cent wage increase, particularly if a similar wage increase is to be paid by the firms which supply its purchased materials and services. And he is likely to have no answer when asked whether he thinks the business will *in fact* absorb the increase without raising prices. The question may not have occurred to him. If it is pointed out that excessive wage increases are in fact not absorbed he is likely to remark on the "greed" of employers.[1]

To be sure, a downward rigidity of selling prices provides

---

[1] In the United States, the profits (before income tax) of "non-financial corporations" normally constitute around 15 per cent of the value of the gross national product originating in such corporations, and the compensation of employees around 65 per cent. Given an average advance of productivity of around 3 per cent a year, a 10 per cent annual wage increase would constitute about a 7 per cent a year increase in unit labour costs. If prices were not raised, a 10 per cent wage increase would thus reduce profits from 15 per cent to about 10½ per cent of the value of output, or by nearly one third. Repeated a second year (again without price increase), profits would fall to about 6 per cent, and in a third year to about 10½ per cent.

Figure 1

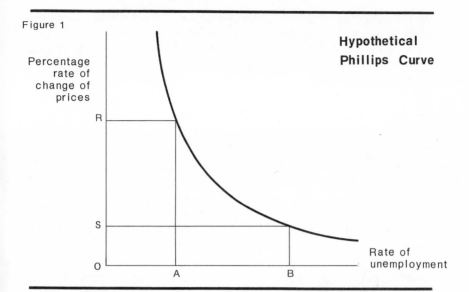

some basis for persistence of the myth that wage increases come only out of profits. In industries which experience rapid increases in productivity, such that moderate wage increases would result in falling unit labour costs, prices are sometimes not reduced sufficiently fully to reflect this, and profit margins are allowed to widen. Although automobile prices in the United States did decline during the late 1950s and early 1960s (mostly through "quality improvements" rather than outright price reductions), they undoubtedly declined by less than unit labour costs. Similarly, the federal agency that regulates airline fares did not require rate reductions to reflect the sharp decline of costs in that industry in the early 1960s. These and similar failures contributed notably to the breakdown of wage stability in the United States in the mid-1960s.

The Phillips Curve analysis

Some of the more systematic portions of the above analysis are frequently summarized in the concept of the so-called Phillips Curve.[1]

In its simplest form, the Phillips Curve idea makes the rate of price increase a function of the extent to which aggregate demand requires the utilization of the economy's productive capacity—as usually measured by the (inverse of the) unemployment rate, or

---

[1] Named after the British economist A. W. Phillips, who first crystalized the concept in a well-known article in *Economica* in 1958.

by the difference between unemployment and vacancies. A simple Phillips Curve is graphically represented as in Figure 1.

In Figure 1, rates of unemployment in excess of OB would be fully consistent with an acceptable stability of prices—a minimal increase of OS per year. But as unemployment fell progressively below OB, the rate of price increase would step up. Rates of unemployment of OA or below would be associated with rapid inflation at the rate of OR per year or higher; and there appears to be no rate of inflation sufficiently high to reduce unemployment to zero—indeed to reduce it much below OA.

Those who use the Phillips Curve may emphasize one or the other (or occasionally both) of the two connections sketched earlier between the degree of unemployment and the rate of inflation: either the explanation that as unemployment declines in response to higher aggregate demand, prices must rise to reflect the intensifying competition among firms for increasingly scarce resources, particularly labour; or the alternative explanation that rising aggregate demand enhances the ability of unions and managements to push up wages and prices. However, the presumed level and shape of the curve might well be affected by one's view of the relative importance of demand-pull and cost elements. But either emphasis provides the theoretical support for a public policy that would attempt to avoid or to cure inflation by restraining aggregate demand.

However, the implications of this policy are now very different from those of the simple "inflationary gap" concept. In that situation, aggregate demand needed to be restrained, in order to avoid inflation, only when it exceeded the maximum physical productive capacity of the economy. Such excess demand was completely "non-functional," and there was no reason not to eliminate it. Now, however, it is seen that there is a "tradeoff": less inflation implies higher unemployment; lower unemployment requires accepting more inflation. And the choice required may be a most painful one: it may be that the level of unemployment (and the personal hardship and social cost thereof) which a society is willing to accept implies a rate of inflation higher than that society can tolerate. Many think that this is the basic dilemma faced by many countries of the Atlantic Community now and in the years ahead.

If this were indeed the dilemma, the only escape would appear to be either to devise and use policy instruments other than those that operate simply through aggregate demand to deal with excessive unemployment or with inflation, or both; or else to find ways of altering the terms of the trade-off, so that they become socially acceptable. However, some economists believe that the assumed invariance of this trade-off relationship is greatly exaggerated. Figure 2 presents a simple empirical counterpart of a Phillips

Figure 2

U.S. Unemployment Rate and Percentage in Prices, 1954-71[1]

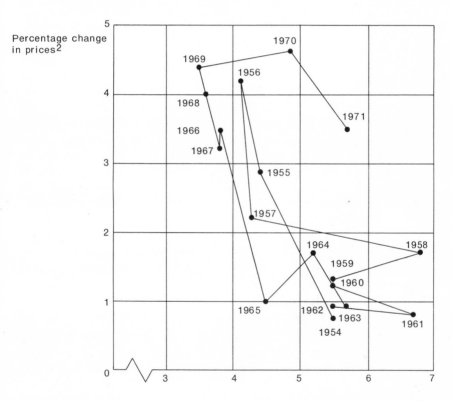

Unemployment rate[3]

Curve for the United States, for the period 1954-1971. Each dot in the quadrant represents one year's experience: measured horizontally, the average level of unemployment during the year, and measured vertically, the change in GNP deflator (for the private non-farm sector of the economy) between the first quarter of that year and the first quarter of the following year. Lines connect each year's observations to the previous and subsequent ones. Data for 1970 are partly estimated, and those for 1971 are the writer's forecasts.

These data demonstrate some rough conformity to the theoretical Phillips Curve model. The years 1954, 1962, and 1963—spanning almost a decade—show almost identical combinations of unemployment rate and price change. But the rate of price increase during 1958 was more than double that of 1961, even though unemployment rates were nearly identical in these two recession years. The price increase during 1955 was almost 3 times as large as that during 1965, with almost the same levels of unemployment; and almost twice as large in 1956 as in 1957, again with very similar unemployment rates. The experience of the years 1955-57 would suggest far more rapid inflation at unemployment rates between 3.5 per cent and 3.8 per cent than was actually experienced in the years 1966-69. And 1970 seems completely out of line with all previous experience shown, as 1971 is almost certain to be. Moreover, observations for post-war years prior to 1954 (although these years admittedly were subject to special factors) bear little apparent relationship to experience during the period 1954-69. Using quarterly data instead of annual, and experimenting with a wide variety of different "lags" between unemployment rate and price change, do not substantially improve the conformity of the relationship to the theoretical model.

The imperfect conformity of observed experience to the theoretical Phillips Curve relationships might have any of several explanations. One explanation is that the Phillips Curve idea, although basically correct, excessively simplifies the rather complex set of forces that produces price level changes in a modern economy. The rate of price change does depend, very importantly, on the level of aggregate demand relative to potential output, of which the rate of unemployment can be taken as a reasonable index. But there are other variables that also must be included in any full explanation of price level changes; and the casual relationships among these variables do not run exclusively in one direction. For example, the level of unemployment mainly explains the rate of change of wages, and thereby of costs and prices. But changes in one set of prices—those which constitute the cost of living—also feed back in helping to determine the rate of change in wages. Prices of farm products and, in most countries, prices of imported goods, which have their own independent causes, significantly affect both the general price level and the cost of living. Changes in prices may also reflect alterations in the rate of productivity advance; changes in the rate of productivity advance also affect the amount of labour required to produce any output and thereby, given the supply of labour, the rate of unemployment. Moreover, each of the relationships may operate with a lag—and possibly a different lag.

Elaborate empirical models have been developed, which incorporate these and other variables, with lags, in a system of equations which simultaneously determines unemployment rates and rates of change in prices. We may call those "extended Phillips Curve" models. It is quite possible to develop such models which are reasonably consistent with past observed experience. Unfortuately, the models so developed have so far proved not to forecast well for subsequent periods. Still, it may be too soon to conclude that the "extended Phillips Curve" approach should be abandoned.

INTERNATIONAL INFLATION:

THE EXPORTING AND IMPORTING OF PRICE LEVELS

The preceding chapter has dealt with the causes of inflation in a single country, as though there were no contact between that country's economy and other economies. Yet international economic interdependence is one of the dominant facts of economic life in the Atlantic Community, and this interdependence clearly extends to the process of inflation. Among the countries of continental Europe, for example, the interdependence of price levels, and hence the interdependence of inflationary developments, differs only in degree from the interdependence of price levels and hence of inflationary developments among the various regions of a single country such as the United States. Through the channels of international trade and payments, it is quite possible for one country to export inflation to others, or for one country to import it from others. The nature of this interdependence needs now to be considered.

The impact of inflation on trade and payments

As a preliminary step to considering the impact of international trade and payments on the extent of a country's inflation, we first consider the impact of a country's inflation on its international trade and payments. We continue to assume—temporarily—that each country's price level is determined entirely by domestic developments and domestic policies and is thus unaffected by all other countries, price levels. For example, assume that a domestic inflation raises prices at home by 10 per cent, while the average price level elsewhere rises by only 5 per cent. Other things being equal, such a rise in domestic prices relative to those elsewhere stimulates the country's demand for imports and reduces other countries' demand for its exports. It will thereby experience a loss of jobs and profits from the decreased production both of export goods and of those domestic goods whose local markets are reduced by rising imports. We will call this the adverse "competitive effect" of a faster rate of inflation. Obviously, there are favourable competitive effects for the country whose prices rise less than elsewhere.

Given rates of inflation at home and abroad, and resulting competitive effects on the physical volumes of the country's imports and exports, its *balance of trade* will be altered—the difference between the money value of its exports and the money value of its imports. For example, it is conceivable (although unlikely) that a domestic inflation could have only a minor restraining effect on the volume of the country's exports, even though its export prices rose considerably; in that case, the money value of its exports could rise appreciably. Similarly, although prices of goods imported from elsewhere rose very little and prices of domestic import substitutes rose a lot, it is conceivable that the volume of imports would be little stimulated; thus the money value of its imports would rise very little. In that case, the country's balance of trade might actually be improved by its inflation. But normally only a moderate rise in prices relative to those abroad will cause a substantial loss of a country's exports and/or a large increase in its imports. In that case—the usual one—the country's trade balance will be impaired by inflation, perhaps seriously.

As a country's trade balance is reduced as a result of its having a higher rate of inflation than elsewhere, it is likely to encounter balance-of-payments problems. Whether it does, and how seriously, will depend on the previous state of its balance of payments, and on what is simultaneously happening to movements of capital between it and other countries. Other things being equal, however, a country which has a prolonged higher-than-average rate of price increase will almost surely, sooner or later, encounter balance-of-payments difficulties. Thus, it is often said there is a "balance-of-payments discipline" which penalizes countries that are unwilling or unable to avoid inflation. They must ultimately "pay the piper" when their international reserves become depleted to the point that they must create a domestic recession, and/or impose welfare-reducing controls on international transactions, and/or devalue their currencies. Those countries which wish to avoid these costs accept the discipline, and do not permit inflation to develop.

Unfortunately, this discipline is not quite as successful in penalizing "sin" and rewarding "virtue" as here described. In the first place, the sin punished is not inflation, but only faster inflation than other countries are experiencing. The implied "code of ethics" is a highly relativist one—it is all right to sin just so long as others are sinning too.

In the second place, there is the equally serious deficiency that the discipline punishes some who have not sinned (i.e., inflated more than others) and fails to punish some others who have. The statement above was that "other things being equal," a country that inflates faster than others will get into trouble. But other things may not always be equal. A country's balance of trade is affected not only by the "competitive effects" associated with price-level changes. It can also be, and often is, heavily affected by any of a large number of other things quite independent of its price levels —which may be happening at the same time. Suppose, for example, that a shift is occurring in buyers' preferences (both those of domestic buyers and of those abroad) as among different kinds of goods. If buyers' preferences at home and abroad are shifting away from rest-of-world products and towards this country's products, its exports may rise and its imports may decline, even though the home economy is experiencing a higher degree of inflation than the rest of the world. In the case of an unfavourable shift in demand, a country's exports may suffer and its imports may increase, even though its prices are more stable than those abroad.

There is a multitude of factors that can explain a (relative) shift of demand from one country's products towards another's. In addition to autonomous changes in consumer tastes, they include changes in the qualities or styles of the goods produced at home and abroad; the introduction of wholly new products at home and abroad that displace others in buyers' patronage; changes in the structure of aggregate demand (including those changes that arise merely from the growth of average incomes) that cause the demand for one set of products (more heavily represented in the exports of one country) to grow faster than the demand for another set of products (more heavily represented in another country's exports); faster, or slower, economic growth in the economies of its trading partners than at home; a country's entry into a preferential trading community (or such entry by countries that provide its principal export markets); and many more such circumstances. Moreover, prices of *specific* export commodities (and specific import-competitive goods) may and sometimes do change quite differently from changes in a country's general price level. For example, even in a country experiencing more inflation than elsewhere, the prices of the particular goods that account for its principal exports or its import substitutes could fall, or rise less than the prices of directly competitive foreign products, because of differing rates of productivity change, or different competitive conditions in the several markets. Thus, the balance of payments discipline may punish some countries that do not inflate, and may fail to punish others that do.

The exporting of inflation through trade

This analysis of the effects of inflation on trade also helps to make clear the effects of trade on inflation, and how one country's inflation may cause another country's price level to rise.

The international transfer of inflation is directly analogous to what happens within the regions of a single country. Casual observation tells us that prices rise (or fall) at roughly the same rate within all the different regions of a large national market like that of the United States. None can get very far out of line. If prices rise faster in the West than in the East, producers in the East find it more profitable to sell in the West, and the inflow of their "exports" controls the rise of Western prices. Likewise, Western producers find it harder to sell in Eastern markets and are forced either to lower their prices or to lose "exports" to the East. Both these responses, however, increase demand and reduce supply in the East and tend to raise prices there. In somewhat attenuated form, the same process works internationally (among countries whose exchange rates are fixed) to keep their price changes at least somewhat in line with each other. The argument will now be developed more fully as it applies to the international case, although it holds even more strongly within a single market.

Assume that, at first, no country is undergoing inflation. Then domestic aggregate demand increases in one country to an extent that threatens to bring about a domestic inflation. This rising pressure of domestic demand will, however, first increase that country's imports from its trading partners, and might, as well, tend to divert some of its own resources from making export goods to production for the home market.

If supplies of imports from other countries were freely available at constant prices, the availability of the imported supplies might fully satisfy the increased demand in the first country, and thereby cushion its price level from any appreciable inflationary pressure. At the same time, however, this process produces an increased pressure of aggregate demand in the economies of its trading partners. The demand for their exports by the first country has increased, while their imports from that country may have decreased (thus reducing the total supply of goods available in their own domestic markets). If aggregate demand was previously deficient and resources unemployed in some or all of the trading partners, the increased demand pressure may be welcome, and thus helpful to them in attaining full employment, just as their increased exports to the first country are helpful to it in avoiding inflation. However, if aggregate demand is, or once it has become, neither deficient nor excessive in the economies of some or all of the trading partners, a strong and persistent rise of demand in the first country could tip the balance towards inflation in many or all of the countries.

It is thus apparent that trade—among countries just as among regions of a single country—is a means by which the pressure of increased demand on supply, wherever it originates, is spread over a larger market, tending thereby to keep the balance between demand and supply relatively similar in all parts of the larger market area. If foreign goods and domestic goods were perfect substitutes one for another, the pressures of demand on supply in one country would be spread evenly over all parts of the trading area, and no part would experience inflation from excessive demand until demand was excessive everywhere and all regions or countries experienced inflation together. Within a single country this is nearly what happens. However, in the separate country case, imports are even less likely to be perfect substitutes for domestic goods than is the case within a country; and imports never are even imperfect substitutes for some domestic activities (e.g., construction and personal services). Thus, excessive demand in one country can begin to create inflation at home even though some or all of the countries with which it trades are not yet at full employment. Even so, as excess demand raises prices at home, the attendant competitive effects will strengthen its "export" of excessive demand to others, and thereby may begin to engender inflation in some of the countries with which the first country's trading relations are closest.

Competitive effects in trade will occur, of course, even if the first country's inflation is entirely of the cost-push variety; and this too could tip the balance of supply and demand in other countries' markets towards inflation.

There have been many cases in recent years in which inflation has clearly been spread from one country (or group of countries) to others through trade effects. This is clearly most important for neighbouring countries which account for an important part of each other's trade, in a volume which is also large relative to one or both countries' domestic production. Excessive demand in the United States in 1966-68, for example, clearly "spilled over" into Canada and had a significant impact on Canada's price levels. During this same period, the strong U.S. demand for imports from Europe and Japan contributed somewhat to rising aggregate demand and to inflationary pressures in those areas. Germany's boom in 1964-65, and again in 1969-70, clearly had strongly inflationary effects on most of her neighbour's economies. Small countries whose trade is large relative to their GNP are almost sure to import any inflation being suffered by their larger neighbours.

Obviously, the reduction of barriers to trade, both multilaterally through GATT and through the formation of EEC and EFTA, has tied countries' economies even more closely together through trade and has made the exporting and importing of inflation between them considerably easier and more significant. Nevertheless, at least in the case of the larger countries, the effects of other countries' inflation on the balance of demand and supply in the home market will rarely have an impact so great or so sudden that it could not be offset by a country that was seriously determined to avoid inflation, and possessed adequate tools for the control of domestic demand.

Just as countries that inflate more rapidly than others export some of their inflation to their neighbours, so those that inflate less rapidly export some of their price stability to others. Countries with stable prices that are able to let their exports to inflating countries grow rapidly tend to hold down others' inflation. Moreover, especially if a country with relatively stable prices has a large internal market—e.g., the United States or Germany—export producers in other countries, ambitious to enter that market or to expand their sales there, have no alternative but to hold down their costs and prices by every possible means. This effort to stabilize their export prices also may help, to some appreciable extent, to stabilize internal costs and prices in their own countries. Though this means, too, that price stability is "exported."

Thus trade effects pull in the direction of keeping price-level changes in all countries relatively similar. Lower rates of inflation tend to be pulled up, higher rates pulled down. However, the pressures towards price-level conformity can rarely be more than partially effective. If domestic policies together with the "export of price stability" by other countries fail to control a particular country's inflation, and its price level gets too far out of line with others', it may ultimately have to bring its international (although not its domestic) price-level back into line by altering its exchange parity. Or, if a country wishes to and is able to achieve substantially greater price stability than its trading partners, it may ultimately have to revalue its currency upwards in order to avoid importing their inflation.

Other ways of exporting inflation

Cost-push Effects. If the prices that must be paid in one country for significant and not easily replaceable imports from another should rise as a result of the other country's inflation, this can set off inflationary impulses in the first country even if there is no change in the aggregate demand for its products. Higher prices paid for essential imported raw materials will raise costs of production and push up the prices of domestic goods made from these materials. Higher prices paid by domestic consumers for such goods, or higher prices for finished consumer goods directly imported, can generate demands for larger wage increases, thus setting off a cost-push spiral. Similar effects may occur as the result of a trading partner's revaluation, or a country's own devaluation.

Such cost-push effects from higher import prices are by themselves unlikely to be decisive, at least in the larger countries. But they can contribute to existing internal cost-push pressures, and intensify an otherwise already difficult problem. Small countries, highly dependent on imports, have no way to resist cost-push inflationary effects from a rise in world market prices.

Labour Migration Effects. The increasingly international labour market that exists in Europe, like that which exists in

North America, provides a further means for the spread of inflation. If the pressure of demand in one country raises wages there and pulls in workers from other countries, this tends to create labour shortages and thereby to raise wage costs in the other countries. The large reservoirs of idle or under-employed workers in Southern Europe and North Africa that were available to meet labour shortages in Northern Europe during the 1960s long helped to cushion the latter region against inflationary pressures, without at the same time creating such pressures in the countries losing workers. Once full (or fuller) employment was achieved in Spain and Italy, rapidly rising aggregate demand in the North was no longer so easily accommodated, and inflationary pressures developed more readily both in the North and the South.

The movement of workers across borders in Northern Europe —among France, Belgium, the Netherlands, Switzerland, and Germany—has also on occasion been in sufficient volume to help to transmit inflationary pressures from rising internal demand from one of these countries to another. Because of the large daily movement of workers across these borders, a wage change on one side must be almost immediately matched on the other.

Imitative effects. In today's increasingly unified world, bound together by massive flows of information through press, radio, television, and the direct observation of tourists, there are still other channels for the importation of inflationary tendencies. (The phrase "importation of inflationary tendencies"—rather than the "export of inflation"—is meant to convey that in this circumstance inflation can be imported even from a country where it does not exist!) Workers in countries in which the growth of productivity is slow see the faster gains in living standards being made by workers elsewhere. When they seek to match those real income gains by securing larger nominal wage increases, in the absence of corresponding productivity gains, this can only create inflation. Some argue that this phenomenon has relevance for the United Kingdom.

Other students have suggested that the wage explosion in Italy in 1970 was in some sense influenced by Italian workers' observations of the events in France in 1968. Here the importation (if any) may have consisted as much of the spirit and tactics of political militancy as of the borrowing of an economic objective. If so, the economic impact of the borrowing was nonetheless inflationary. It may be, of course, that both wage explosions (and those in other countries) reflect common social and political trends of wider origin.

On the other hand, some have suggested that, during the early part of the 1960s, the excellent price performance of the United States had a widespread dampening effect on price expectations— and thus, indirectly, on inflation—throughout the Atlantic world, an effect that has now been lost.

Direct investment effects. A country involved in an inflation-boom may find its problems of controlling demand intensified by the participation of foreign entrepreneurs in its investment boom. An inflationary impact is not, however, the inevitable result of foreign direct investment. Foreign direct investment will be inflationary primarily to the extent that (a) it results in a larger total volume of investment than would otherwise have occurred through domestic entrepreneurial activity alone, and (b) this increased total investment is not offset by foreign entrepreneurs' greater importation of capital goods. If foreign entrepreneurs merely make investments that would otherwise have been made by domestic firms, or if their extra volume of investment is matched by their importation of capital goods from their home countries, it need not be inflationary: indeed, in the latter case, it may thereafter be an anti-inflationary influence. Even if foreign direct investment were inflationary in the first instance, the importation of more advanced technology that might accompany the foreign investment could subsequently permit a faster expansion of output with less strain on domestic resources and thus, again, subsequently help to cushion the country against inflationary tendencies.

The impacts of foreign direct investment are many and it raises many issues more important than that of its contribution to inflationary pressures. Nevertheless, under some circumstances it might contribute to inflation, and it is possible that it has sometimes done so in the Atlantic Community during the post-war period.

The impacts of capital flows

Almost no subject in recent years has stirred more controversy than that of the impacts of the international flows of "liquid capital" and "portfolio investment." Such flows have been massive in recent years in the Atlantic Community. They have responded to interest-rate differentials, to speculation over revaluations or devaluations of currencies, and in some instances to tax changes or efforts to escape taxation. They often have been described as a mechanism through which inflation is exported along with the capital. More appropriately, we should call it a means by which inflation is imported along with the capital, for the capital-exporting country need not be one suffering inflation.

However, such flows do not *directly* affect aggregate demand or cost pressures either in the exporting or the importing country. Yet they may do so indirectly if they—along with the financial flows associated with the net balance on trade, tourism, services, and other international transactions—affect credit availability and/or interest rates in either country through altering its domestic supply of money and credit. In some countries—e.g., the United States—the central bank can without difficulty completely insulate domestic monetary conditions from the financial effects of balance of payments surpluses or deficits, and almost invariably does so, mainly through open-market operations. This is not the case in many other countries, and it would require institutional changes to provide the machinery necessary to permit their central banks to accomplish that insulation.

The case for *not* insulating domestic monetary conditions from capital flows would rest on a presumption that all international flows of foreign exchange respond to basic economic forces which make domestic monetary expansion appropriate when funds flow in and monetary contraction appropriate when funds flow out. If a country experiences an increase in international reserves as the result of its own export boom, occasioned by the fact that its price level is "too low" relative to other countries' prices, an expansionary monetary policy might conceivably be deemed appropriate to create the inflationary conditions at home which would restore equilibrium in its balance of payments—although few governments or central banks might reach that conclusion. In the opposite case, however, in which reserves decrease as a result of an import surplus because domestic prices are rising in response to excessive demand, it might well be appropriate if this loss of reserves automatically brought about a deflationary monetary policy. In this case, the balance of payments discipline would be working—quite automatically—in the direction it is supposed to work, namely to restrain an inappropriate inflation.

But none of this has much relevance to those changes in reserves which result primarily from capital flows. If, for example, the importation of capital is attracted by high interest rates which were deliberately raised by a restrictive domestic monetary policy in order to fight a domestic inflation, an increase in the country's money supply arising from capital imports does not thereby become appropriate. Indeed, its effects are precisely counter to the original objective. If the import of capital occurs because another country is using an easy money policy to stimulate its domestic economy, which lowers its domestic interest rates and causes funds to flow out, this fact does not itself make monetary expansion appropriate in countries which are the recipients of such outflows. Nor is there any significant *a priori* case showing that fund inflows or outflows relating to speculation about changes in exchange parities (other than perhaps the country's own) provide any clear guidance as to what internal monetary policy is appropriate.

There was once an economic theory that related to an (even then) probably non-existent world: one in which all prices and wages were perfectly flexible, in which no government needed to use nor tried to use nor would be able to use domestic monetary policy as an instrument of economic stabilization, and in which the international money—gold—was also the sole circulating domestic money. For such a world, there was a theory about how international interest rate differentials reflected only the relative abundance or scarcity of capital and the relative availability of opportunities for profitable investment in various countries; and how capital flows that responded to these interest rate differentials generated price differentials that in turn generated flows of exports and imports that maximized welfare all around. That world bears little relationship to the one we know.

In our world, one or more of several changes would appear to be necessary in order to deal effectively with problems of the international transmission of inflation (or deflation) through undesired flows of capital. One would be for all important countries (or groups of countries participating in a community that seeks to carry out a common monetary policy) to develop effective means to insulate their domestic monetary systems from international inflows or outflows of funds. In this way they could more effectively use monetary policy to deal with problems of domestic economic instability. A quite different solution would be for major countries to coordinate more effectively their monetary policies so as to minimize undesired and destabilizing capital flows, while encouraging capital flows that promote balance of payments equilibrium both in countries exporting and countries importing the capital. However, this would require that countries should have and be able to use tools other than monetary policy to deal with problems of internal stability—most importantly, flexible fiscal policies. A third solution would be "floating" exchange rates, or new and easier means for exchange parities to be adjusted frequently and in small amounts. Other solutions are perhaps possible, including direct controls on capital flows, controls on the receipt or payment of interest, or perhaps flexible tax mechanisms. However, the analysis and solution of today's balance of payments problems—which only in part arise from inflation—lie entirely beyond the scope of this paper.

The export and import of price stability

The preceding pages have suggested a number of ways in which inflationary tendencies may be—and often are—transferred across international borders in the Atlantic Community. However, in most cases, this is a reciprocal process: these are also ways in which price stability can be transferred across international borders: the means by which inflation in one country is restrained by relative stability in another. And indeed this has often happened.

Until 1965, and particularly between 1960 and 1965, the United States economy (and that of Canada) constituted an "island of stability" in a world in which many countries experienced strong tendencies towards inflation. Much of the time in the past 15 years, Germany, and, at least in important product lines, Italy and Japan, have also been strong forces for stability, absorbing inflationary pressures originating elsewhere rather than radiating such pressures to others. The reservoirs of unemployed or under-employed labour in Southern Europe were for many years, and to some extent remain, another great force for stability.

Surely, price stability—just as inflation—is an exportable commodity, even though there is now perhaps less of it around to export. But even when there was more of it on the market, it is probable that the international pressures towards stability and towards inflation were not fully symmetrical. Why?

Partly it is merely the "ratchet effect," the fact that wages and prices go up far more easily than down. Today, international variation in price level performance exists only on one side of zero change; domestic price levels do not decline (although a country's international prices may decline through devaluation). Moreover, ratchet effects mean that it is easier for the countries with inflation to export that inflation to others than to import the others' stability.

Second, many of the ways in which one country can export stability to others require that it have a margin of idle resources—so that it can readily increase its exports of goods—and/or of labour—to satisfy excessive demand pressures elsewhere. Today countries are both more ambitious in their employment objectives and better able to achieve them. Thus there are typically (and progressively) fewer circumstances in which some countries are in a position to export stability to others.

Third, the alleged discipline of the balance of payments, which is one instrument through which the stable countries export their stability to others, has increasingly been seen to be a captious and often misdirected master. Countries may have balance of payments difficulties even though their inflation is considerably less than that experienced elsewhere—as was the case, for example, for the United States, between 1955 and 1965. Other countries have experienced more than the average rate of inflation, yet have been saved from trouble through demand shifts or fortunate capital flows. Recognition of these facts has led to the development of new international machinery, and of new attitudes, that have in effect relaxed the balance of payments discipline, even when that discipline is properly exerted on countries which get into trouble through inflation.

Countries experiencing less inflation than others, whether or not this is reflected in an improved balance of payments, surely do not invite inflation nor willingly accept it. But the control of inflation is almost always difficult, unpleasant, painful. If a country's price record up to now has been better than average, and its balance of payments is favourable, it finds it easier to postpone efforts to avoid or control new impulse to inflation in the hope that the problem will go away, or to relax its efforts to avoid or control inflation once they begin to show partial results. But countries with poorer price records do not thereby find their efforts to control inflation any more pleasant or less painful. They do what they think they can do. And their task is not easier simply because other countries, whose past price records are better, are more relaxed about dealing with their own inflationary pressures. Indeed, the task of the countries in trouble is made *more difficult* by the other countries' reduced ability to export price stability.

AN INFORMAL CLASSICAL MODEL OF THE
CURRENT ECONOMIC DEVELOPMENT PROBLEM

HARRY G. JOHNSON

For over two decades the economically advanced countries of the western world, particularly the United States, have been concerned with promoting the economic development of poorer countries. Since the early 1960s however, there has been growing disillusionment with the progress achieved so far. Recently the Pearson Report, *Partners in Development,* has called attention to a number of serious problems confronting the global development effort in the next decade. These problems include the population explosion; growing urban unemployment; concern with the inappropriateness of western industrial technology as applied to the conditions of relative abundance of labor and scarcity of capital in the developing countries (with a complementary emphasis on the need to develop more appropriate technologies); and the judgment that the promotion of economic development as practiced so far has not lessened, but may have even increased, inequality in the distribution of income and wealth, with serious effects on the political stability necessary for modernizing a society and economy, and attaining orderly economic development.

The purpose of this paper is to suggest that these phenomena are logically connected and can be explained by a rather simple theoretical model. This model draws heavily on the early classic article of Arthur Lewis, "Economic Development with Unlimited Supplies of Labor," but goes beyond that model in developing an analysis of its implications for unemployment and inequality of income distribution, and also in pointing to alternatives to Lewis's proposed solution of the poverty problem through increasing productivity in the subsistence sector. In so doing, it employs ideas derived from a still earlier and unduly neglected paper by R. F. Kahn. The model is described as "classical" for two reasons: its foundation on the Lewis model, whose approach is classical in the "history-of-thought" meaning of the term; and its assumption of rationality in behavioral responses to economic incentives. The particular form given to the latter I owe to the work of my colleague at the University of Chicago, Arnold C. Harberger. The model is described as "informal" because I do not attempt to develop an explicit dynamic general equilibrium model of the development process, but only to indicate the key elements of such a model. I shall try, however, to indicate the points at which the more elaborate model would need to be closed.

The starting point of the model is Lewis's two assumptions: that there is an unlimited supply of labor available at a specific wage in the subsistence sector, and that the wage rate in the industrial sector exceeds that in the subsistence sector by a conventional margin greater than the excess costs of urban living as compared with subsistence-sector living. In contrast to Lewis's work, however, it is emphasized that the assumption of unlimited labor-availability assumes a dynamics of population growth according to which labor breeds to the level of subsistence. This assumption has the important implication that an increase in the subsistence wage cannot be obtained simply by improving the technology of production in the subsistence sector. Any such improvement by itself will merely enlarge the population in the subsistence sector, and benefits may be assumed to accrue to the owners of land or natural resources, which may be assumed to be the factor of production in inelastic supply in that sector. The fact that on the assumption of an unlimited labor supply at a constant subsistence wage the benefits of technical progress will accure entirely to land-owners implies, given the usual circumstances of unequal initial shares of land ownership and differential propensities to refrain from consumption in order to accumulate land holdings, that such technical progress will produce a growing inequality in the distribution of income from agricultural activity, and consequently growing political unrest and agitation for land reform. This part of the story, however, will not be developed further here. The point relevant to the present analysis is that an increase in the real subsistence wage requires a constriction of the population, either absolutely in relation to the available natural resources in the absence of technical progress, or relatively in relation to the rate of technical progress in a subsistence sector. The problem is that, except in the case of a purely peasant agriculture, the social gain from population restraint (in terms of average standard of living) is not reflected in private incentives to population limitation, since reduction of procreativity by any individual family will simply permit the survival of more children born to other families. A further interesting possibility is also neglected, though its implications in the model can easily be worked out—that improved medical care provided at public expense will reduce the level of the subsistence wage to which the population breeds.

Lewis's second assumption is the existence of a conventional margin of urban industrial wages over farm earnings. Part of the observed margin represents the higher real costs of urban life as compared with rural. This margin will be ignored in what follows. The artificial part of the margin can be explained in two ways. The first is that rural labor obtains an average share of agricultural or subsistence sector output, including a share of the part attributable to the rent on natural resources. This explanation is dependent on the supplementary hypothesis either of a land-owning peasant with an equalitarian family structure or of social restrictions on landlords requiring them to share some part of their rents with their tenants. Either case is implausible as an approximation of the typical land-holding situation of the developing countries. Hence, it also will be ignored in what follows. The alternative explanation is that, for various reasons, the industrial sector finds it profitable to pay wages above the alternative opportunity cost of the relevant labor in the rural sector.

There are three reasons that may be mentioned, each having different implications. The first is that industry finds it worthwhile to pay a premium wage in order to have its pick of the available labor force to ensure maximum physical and mental efficiency of those workers it hires—the traditional "economy of high wages" argument. The second reason is that management may wish to maintain community or political goodwill. The third is that it may wish to ensure the availability of a labor force large enough to satisfy peak demands. These motivations are common enough in the industrial history of western countries (witness labor practices on the docks, and more recently, those in the automotive industry). They should not occasion surprise in the less developed countries, where a reliable labor force is likely to be a far more economically advantageous industrial asset than it would be in the advanced industrial countries.

On the first explanation, the industrial wage differential over the subsistence sector wage is a necessary economic cost of industrial efficiency in a backward environment. Its incidental effects—income inequality and unemployment—are part of the price of economic development.

The second explanation is that some combination of the political power of organized labor and socialist ideas favouring trade unionism, "fair" industrial wages, and social security, insists that industrial labor be paid a wage (including fringe benefits in the form of "decent" working conditions, and social security rights) above the alternative opportunity cost of labor in the subsistence sector. In this case, the wage differential is not an economic cost of doing business in an under-developed economy, but a tax imposed by the political environment on the process of economic development.

The third explanation is that, as a legacy of past colonial rule, civil service and industrial pay scales continue to be set at levels designed to attract educated westerners to an expatriate existence. This situation also involves a political tax on industrial development, but in this case it is a tax favoring an educated class rather than organized labor. This explanation carries more serious social and economic implications than the ones previously described, for the key to entry into this kind of pay system is educational attainment. This involves a much smaller investment of resources for natives than for foreigners, but it is, nevertheless, a substantial investment in local terms. The investment required places a demand on scarce local capital resources and manifests itself politically as a demand for free or subsidized higher education (on a level above the capacity of the economy to absorb its products), and for the deterioration of educational standards to permit more candidates to obtain the formal qualifications demanded of job applicants. This condition results in an educational surplus deficient in quality, and a misallocation of national resources. (By contrast, the monopoly privileges for acceptable members of the labor force discussed in the previous two cases involve discrimination among individuals and inequity of income distribution but are not necessarily a waste of resources). Further, the sharp discrimination in incomes and social status between those who are marginal educational successes and obtain high-paid jobs, and those who are marginal educational failures and have to make do with inferior careers, and the presence in the society of a body of students temporarily pampered by society but deeply worried about whether they will succeed (thus critical and envious of those who have) and of a group of educational failures educated beyond their eventual status in life, are potent sources of political unrest. Even in advanced industrial societies, which have a greater capacity to absorb people of differing standards of university-level achievement, it has been evident that the control of access to the better jobs by educational requirements combined with the "democratic" practice of subsidized university education to those possessing the prior qualification for it, makes at least a substantial minority of the student body a potential source of disruptive political activity. Whatever the reason for the conventional wage differential (and hereafter I abstract from the higher costs of urban life, the real elements in the "economy of high wages," and the cost of acquiring economically necessary educational qualifications), its effects are predictable from conventional economic theory in two ways.

First, the conventional theory of production implies that entrepreneurs will choose a more capital-intensive and technology-intensive method of production than is appropriate for the true social alternative opportunity cost of labor. (Another way of putting this point, favored by Harberger, is to say that the wage rate does in fact measure the alternative opportunity cost of labor in the economy because of the unemployment the wage differential generates). In consequence of this rational choice by entrepreneurs, there will naturally be dissatisfaction over the failure of industrial growth and investment in industrial capital to generate as much employment as expected, complaints that the technology employed is inappropriate to local relative factor prices, and demands that it be modified so as to become more labor-intensive. In the popular mind, the entrepreneur's choice of technology is regarded as a wilful slavishness to western methods, which he should be forced by political pressure to recant for the public good. At a more sophisticated level, new technology is recognized as requiring an investment by someone, and the obvious candidate (vide the Pearson Report) is western development assistance. In neither case, however, has the influence of labor-pricing policies in choice of techniques been adequately appreciated.

Second, and more important because more subtle, the standard theory of choice under conditions of uncertainty implies that the conventional wage differential will necessarily create urban unemployment. Faced with the choice of a career in the subsistence sector, with a certain but low real income, and highly-paid industrial employment which carries a risk of initial or recurrent temporary unemployment, labor will tend to move from the subsistence sector into the industrial sector until the probability of unemployment in the latter rises to the point at which the prospective net advantages of urban existence are no more attractive than those in the subsistence sector.

The equilibrium rate of unemployment required for this condition will depend on two factors. First, as the theory of choice under uncertainty has made clear, if the average laborer is a risk-averter, prepared to sacrifice prospective average income for the sake of security, the expectation of income in the industrial sector, allowing for unemployment, must be higher than the subsistence wage. Conversely, if the average laborer is a risk-taker, prepared to sacrifice expected income for the sake of a chance of high income, the expectation of income in the industrial sector, allowing for unemployment, will be lower than the subsistence wage. One might venture the conjecture on the basis of the literature on young men and women who leave the farm to seek their fortunes in the city, that in developing economies, with a relatively small urban-industrial sector, the industrial sector will be dominated by the risk-takers.

Second, the recently emerging theory of public goods suggests that occupational and locational choices are influenced not merely by private income opportunities but also by the availability of costless utility-yielding amenities and entertainments. Since the average person in a developing country cannot afford possession of the instruments of instant communication and mass transport (telephones, radios, television, and private automobiles) which enable people in more advanced countries to remain in touch with each other and with civilization while living in remote areas, the attractions of urban life are presumably much stronger in a less developed country than in an advanced one. A further consideration in this vein is that city life offers a greater range of private choice in the expenditure of income than does life in the country, so that more utility can be derived from a smaller measured income than is possible in the subsistence sector. The implication of both these factors is that an industrial wage-differential will generate far more urban unemployment in a developing country than it would in an industrially advanced country.

The central point in the foregoing analysis is the positive functional relationship between the industrial-subsistence sectoral wage differential and the unemployment rate. This relationship has direct implication on the question of inequality of income distribution, especially if one identifies politically relevant inequality with inequality as perceived by the urban population. The higher the wage differential, the larger the proportion of the urban population that will be living with frustrated expectations of a relatively high income. The higher the wage differential, the larger the number of unemployed, the higher the income that they could but do not have, and the higher the cost of the luxury goods of industrial life.

There are other, more indirect but still important, connections between the wage differential and the perceived inequality of income distribution. In order to construct a model of them, it is necessary to make further assumptions about industrial competition and pricing. The simplest assumption is that government policy, with respect to the protection and stimulation of industrial activity, guarantees prices for industrial products sufficiently high to provide a certain minimum real return in the form of goods and services per unit of capital employed in the industrial sector. Both capitalists and workers in the industrial sector may be assumed to spend their incomes partly on industrial products, and partly on the direct or indirect products of the subsistence sector. (Note that this assumption implicitly ignores the problem of subsistence sector demand for industrial goods.) The indirect products of the subsistence sector are conceived of as the services and products rendered within the urban sector by people who migrate from rural areas and are prepared to work for regular wages at the subsistence-sector level. The existence of these people involves a kind of multiplier relationship between the industrial labor force, both employed and unmployed, and the total urban labor force. So there is at all times: (1) a given stock of capital guaranteed its minimum rate of return in real terms; (2) an employed industrial labor force, the number of which is determined by the capital stock and the industrial wage level (or the wage differential); (3) an unemployed industrial labor force, determined by the wage differential and the labor supply preference factors previously discussed; and (4) a service and handicraft urban sector determined by the proportions in which industrial capitalists and labor distribute the expenditure of industrial income among industrial products, urban non-industrial products and services, and subsistence sector goods. A higher wage differential implies: (1) no change in the real income of the capitalists; (2) an increase in the real income but a reduction of the numbers of the industrially employed; (3) an increase in the number of the industrially unemployed; and (4) through a shift in demand towards non-industrial goods and services (induced by the rise in price of industrial products because of the higher cost of industrial labor without a compensating reduction in capitalists' profits) an increase in the ratio of the non-industrial to the industrial urban labor force. The result must be an increase in the perceived inequality of urban income distribution, for not only do capitalists' incomes remain unchanged and the incomes of the industrially-employed increase, but also the ratio of the industrially-unemployed and the urban non-industrial subsistence-wage labor force to the industrially-employed increases. (The exceptional possibility is that because of a high elasticity of substitution between labor and capital in production in the industrial sector, and a low elasticity of substitution between industrial and urban non-industrial goods in the consumption of capitalists and the industrially employed, the total number of unemployed workers and non-industrial urban workers falls.)

The foregoing analysis is couched in comparatively static terms. The outline of an analysis of the effects of economic growth on technology, unemployment, and income inequality is, however, already clear. Sheer accumulation of capital, at a constant rate of return, (technology and the wage differential remaining unchanged) will merely expand the industrial and urban sectors of the economy, and possibly the subsistence sector also (to the extent that its size depends on the urban demand for its products in exchange for industrial goods.) However, what happens to the personal distribution of income and its inequality will depend on whether or not the accumulation of capital is the result of saving by existing capitalists or the emergence of new capitalists. The assumption in developing countries is that much of the accumulation of capital will be conducted by existing capitalists, so that economic development will involve mounting disparities in the distribution of income between capitalists and workers. On the assumption that capital accumulation requires a rising income for capitalists per unit of capital invested (in order to induce them to undertake the increasing risks of investment in more ambitious industrial ventures) income inequality will increase unless the number of capitalists increases faster than the amount of capital. On the assumption that capitalists enjoy a constant real income per unit of capital invested, but that over time the wage differential is steadily increased, the result must be increasing inequality of income distribution, with the possible two exceptions previously mentioned—a high elasticity of substitution between labor and capital in the industrial sector, or a low elasticity of substitution between industrial and subsistence urban goods. A third exception would be a steady reduction in the average capital of the individual capitalist.

Assuming a fixed wage differential and fixed income per unit of capital invested, general technical progress would tend to reduce inequality of income distribution in the urban sector in two ways: by increasing employment per unit of capital (though the unemployment ratio would remain constant), and by reducing the ratio of non-industrial urban labor to the industrial labor force through a reduction of the relative price of industrial goods as compared to goods and services provided by the urban subsistence sector.

At the other extreme, if industrial wages rose proportionately with technical progress, and industrial prices remained constant in terms of subsistence sector prices, the percentage of industrial unemployment would steadily rise, while the ratio of the urban non-industrial to the urban industrial labor force would remain constant. Thus, inequality would increase. A more detailed examination of the effects of technical progress obviously requires a more precise examination of its nature, which is beyond the scope of this essay.

The main conclusions emerging from this analysis of the current problems of economic development are the following: first, contrary to the recommendations of Arthur Lewis, improvement in the technology of the subsistence sector is not a solution, unless "improvement of productivity" is meant as both an improvement in technology and the application of a population control policy sufficiently effective to translate that improvement into an increase in subsistence-sector real wages. In terms of greater equality of income-distribution, subsistence-sector wages must rise relative to industrial-sector wages. Second, the recommendation of Raul Prebisch and others for an accelerated program of industrialization to provide more urban industrial employment, will not solve the problem as long as population breeds to the level of subsistence. The only hope for a crash program of industrialization succeeding is that by temporarily raising subsistence-sector incomes it will raise the long-run real supply price of population (the minimum real wage in the subsistence sector), by inducing more stringent population control practices. Third, a determined effort to reduce the conventional industrial-subsistence wage differential—which would require a reversal of important and deeply-rooted political attitudes and industrial practices—could do much to mitigate the problems of urban unemployment and inequality of income distribution that currently trouble the developing world.

REFERENCES

1. W. Arthur Lewis. "Economic Development with Unlimited Supplies of Labor," *The Manchester School,* Vo. 22, No. 3 (May 1954), pp. 139-91.

2. R. F. Kahn. "The Pace of Development," *The Challenge of Development* (Eliezer Kaplan School of Economics and Social Sciences, The Hebrew University of Jerusalem, 1958), pp. 163-98.

POSTWAR JAPANESE GROWTH AND
THE HARROD-DOMAR MODEL

MARTIN BRONFENBRENNER

I

The Harrod-Domar growth model is a useful instrument to examine the economic growth of a country and to specify the conditions under which growth can be promoted. Our attempt here is to use the model to look into the secrets of rapid Japanese postwar economic growth in particular and to speculate on its future prospects.

Two approaches are combined in this model: that of Sir Roy Harrod and that of E. D. Domar. Each starts with different assumptions, but they come to the same conclusions.

The Harrod model, which appeared originally in 1939,[1] assumes that the expansion path of income in the economy is stable as long as planned savings are equal to planned investment at all points in time. From this assumption, a set of equations (1-3) is generated:

$$S = \alpha Y \tag{1}$$

where α is the marginal and average propensity to save, Y is income, and S is planned savings. Equation (1) says that planned savings constitute a fixed portion of income.

$$I = \beta \frac{dY}{dt} \tag{2}$$

where I is planned investment, β is a coefficient, and t is time. Equation (2) says that planned investment is related to the change of income over time. ("Planned investment" here refers to the investment net of depreciation, and not the gross investment. The gross investment is never negative, but the net planned investment can be negative if income falls.)

70

The equilibrium condition is one in which planned savings equal planned investment:

$$\alpha Y = \beta \frac{dY}{dt} \qquad (3)$$

which can be re-written

$$\alpha Y - \beta \frac{dY}{dt} = 0. \qquad (4)$$

Equation (4) is a simple differential equation which yields the solution:

$$\ln Y - \frac{\alpha}{\beta} t = \ln Y_0 \qquad (5)$$

where Y_0 is an initial level of income.

Taking antilogarithms, equation (5) can be transformed into the following exponential equation:

$$Y = Y_0 e^{\frac{\alpha}{\beta} t} \qquad (6)$$

Equation (6) says that under the condition in which planned savings and planned investment are equal, the equilibrium income grows at the rate α/β. From equation (6), we can derive the planned savings and the planned investment functions.

$$S = \alpha Y = \alpha Y_0 e^{\frac{\alpha}{\beta} t} \qquad (7)$$

$$I = \beta \frac{dY}{dt} = \beta Y_0 e^{\frac{\alpha}{\beta} t} \left(\frac{\alpha}{\beta}\right) = \alpha Y_0 e^{\frac{\alpha}{\beta} t} \qquad (8)$$

As expected, the two results (7-8) are identical.

The Domar model (dating from 1946)[2] starts with a different approach. It is assumed that the equilibrium path of income in the economy requires that the income effect of investment be equal to its output effect. The income effect is:

$$k = \frac{dY}{dI} = \frac{1}{\alpha} \qquad (9)$$

where k is a *multiplier* defined as the change of income due to a change in investment. Equation (9) says that the multiplier is equal to one over the marginal propensity to save. From equation (9), we find:

$$\frac{dY}{dI} = \frac{dY}{dt} / \frac{dI}{dt} = \frac{1}{\alpha} \qquad (10)$$

$$\frac{dY}{dt} = \frac{1}{\alpha} \frac{dI}{dt}. \qquad (11)$$

Equation (11) indicates the income effect of investment

Let σ be the incremental income-capital ratio, defined as follows:

$$\sigma = \frac{dY}{dK} . \qquad (12)$$

By definition, net investment is the change of capital over time:

$$I = \frac{dK}{dt} . \qquad (13)$$

From equations (12) and (13):

$$\frac{dY}{dt} = \frac{dY}{dK} \frac{dK}{dt} = I\sigma . \qquad (14)$$

Equation (14) indicates the output effect of investment.

The equilibrium condition calls for the income and the output effects of investment to be in balance. Therefore, by equations (11) and (14), we find: $I\sigma = \frac{1}{a} \frac{dI}{dt}$,

which can be re-written as the following differential equation:

$$I\sigma - \frac{1}{a} \frac{dI}{dt} = 0 . \qquad (15)$$

Equation (15) yields the following solution:

$$\ln I - a\sigma t = \ln I_o, \qquad (16)$$

where   is an initial level of investment. Taking antilogarithms, equation (16) can be transformed into an exponential equation:

$$I = I_o e^{a\sigma t} . \qquad (17)$$

Again assuming planned saving equal to planned investment,

$$Y = \frac{S}{a} = \frac{I}{a} = \frac{I_o}{a} e^{a\sigma t} = Y_o e^{a\sigma t} . \qquad (18)$$

Equation (18) of the Domar model is the same as equation (6) of the Harrod model, because

$$\sigma = \frac{1}{\beta} = \frac{dY}{dK} .$$

The expansion path of equilibrium income follows an exponential curve starting from Y_o, and grows at the rate of a/β or $a\sigma$ This equilibrium path is unstable. If the expansion path of income should depart from the curve, it will not return to the curve on its own. There is no invisible hand to guide the growth of income to the equilibrium path, and government intervention is in order.

The instability of the model can be shown as follows: assuming the actual income, Y, to be either greater or smaller than the equilibrium income Y_e,

$$(19)$$

The logarithmic expression of equation (19) is $Y \gtrless Y_e = Y_o e^{\frac{\alpha}{\beta} t}$

$$\ln Y \gtrless \ln Y_o + \frac{\alpha}{\beta} t . \qquad (20)$$

Differentiate equation (20) with respect to time, and

$$\frac{dY/dt}{Y} \gtrless \frac{\alpha}{\beta} . \qquad (21)$$

Equation (21) is multiplied by βY,

$$\beta \frac{dY}{dt} \gtrless \alpha Y,$$

the direction of the inequality remaining unchanged because both β and Y are positive.

Equation (22) says that if the actual Y is greater than the equilibrium Y_e, the planned investment generated will be greater than the planned saving, so that the actual Y in the next period will diverge even further from the equilibrium Y_e. By the same reasoning, if the actual Y is smaller than the equilibrium Y_e, the actual Y in the next period will fall even further short of the equilibrium Y_e. Keeping the income growth on the equilibrium expansion path is like balancing on the edge of a knife, and government intervention from time to time is unavoidable.

The same conclusion holds for the Domar model. Assuming planned investment to be greater or smaller than the equilibrium investment I_e:

$$I \gtrless I_e = I_o e^{\alpha \sigma t} . \qquad (23)$$

The logarithmic expression of equation (23) is

$$\ln I \gtrless \ln I_o + \alpha \sigma t \qquad (24)$$

Differentiate equation (24) with respect to time, and

$$\frac{dI/dt}{I} \gtrless \alpha \sigma . \qquad (25)$$

Equation (25) is multiplied by α, and divided by I

$$\frac{dI/dt}{\alpha} \gtrless I \sigma . \qquad (26)$$

The direction of the inequality remains unchanged, because both I and α are positive.

Equation (26) indicates that if planned investment is greater than equilibrium I_e, the income effect of investment will be greater than the output effect of investment. This makes the investment in the next period diverge further from the equilibrium investment.

A word of explanation is necessary regarding the model. Here α is the average and the marginal propensity to save, or one minus the average (or marginal) propensity to consume. The question is: can the average propensity to consume and the marginal propensity to consume be assumed to be equal? In the short run the two are different, but in the long run, (over periods of ten years or more) the two are quite close to each other. As for σ it is the change of income due to a change of capital. In mathematical terms, it is the total derivative of income with respect to capital, or the inverse of the capital-output ratio.

II

The Harrod-Domar model concentrates on the saving-investment process (on the demand side) as the major determining factor of economic growth. A rival model, the neo-classical, concentrates instead upon the supply of goods, leaving demand to the care of fiscal or monetary policy at each stage. In explaining an actual case, such as postwar Japanese economic growth, we find it desirable to use elements from both models. From the Harrod-Domar model one can extract the threat of instability as a rationalization for constant government and quasi-monopoly interference with the development process.[3] From the neo-classical model one can extract the importance of total employment (N) and of labor productivity. Both models agree upon stressing the total capital stock (K) and its productivity.[4]

In the neo-classical model, income is assumed to be determined by a production function of the capital stock and the volume of employment: $Y = f(N,K)$,

$$(27)$$

whose total differential, dY, can be written:

$$dY = \frac{\partial Y}{\partial N} dN + \frac{\partial Y}{\partial K} dK . \quad (28)$$

Equation (28) states that the change Y comes in two ways: the first term implies change stemming from the labor effect, and the second term change stemming from the capital effect. There are altogether four factors to determine the change of income: dK and dN are the changes in inputs of labor and capital, and $\partial Y/\partial N$ and $\partial Y/\partial K$ represent the effectiveness of the resources—that is the marginal product of labor and the marginal product of capital.

Equation (28) is divided by Y,

$$\frac{dY}{Y} = (\frac{\partial Y}{\partial N} \frac{1}{Y}) dN + (\frac{\partial Y}{\partial K} \frac{1}{Y}) dK. \quad (29)$$

Multiply both the numerator and the denominator of the first term on the right by N and those of the second term by K:

$$\frac{dY}{Y} = (\frac{\partial Y}{\partial N} \frac{N}{Y}) \frac{dN}{N} + (\frac{\partial Y}{\partial K} \frac{K}{Y}) \frac{dK}{K} . \qquad (30)$$

Equation (30) can be condensed into

$$G_Y = S_N G_N + S_K G_K, \qquad (31)$$

where G_Y stands for dY/Y, the growth rate of Y; G_N stands for dN/N,ı the growth rate of N; and G_K stands for dK/K, the growth rate of K. S_N represents $\frac{\partial Y}{\partial N} \frac{N}{Y}$, which is the ratio of the percentage change of Y due to the percentage change of N or the employment elasticity of income. Similarly, S_K is the capital elasticity of income.

From this model, there appear to be several ways to improve the growth of income: first, by an increase in the growth rate of capital, G_K, through the savings and investment process as called for by the original model; second, by an increase in the growth rate of employment, G_N; and third, by an improvement of the effectiveness of the inputs, S_N and S_K.

With income being a function of employment and capital, the factor σ of the Domar model can be expanded as follows:

$$\sigma = \frac{dY}{dK} = \frac{\partial Y}{\partial K} + \frac{\partial Y}{\partial N} \frac{dN}{dK} . \qquad (32)$$

Equation (32) says that the income effect of capital, σ has two parts. The first part, $\partial Y/\partial K$, is the marginal product of capital, and can be referred to as the direct effect. The second part, $\frac{\partial Y}{\partial N} \frac{dN}{dK}$, is the income effect of capital through the change in employment, and can be referred to as an indirect effect. The second part implies a chain reaction: for a given change in capital, there will be a change in employment, and because of the change in employment, there will be a change in income.

This theory of economic development deals largely with methods of increasing the growth-rate of income. Here the Japanese have done better than many other countries. There are three secrets to their success.

The first is to keep a high. A high a which is the savings ratio S/Y, will help to generate a high rate of growth of income. However, high a alone is not enough. A high saving ratio associated with a low investment demand is more likely to cause economic stagnation than economic growth.

The second secret is to keep σ high, which means to make capital work efficiently. This involves two steps. The first is to develop technology which will keep the capital-output ratio low, or the marginal product of capital high—as per $\delta Y / \delta K$, the first term of equation (32). Keeping the capital-output ratio low depends a great deal on the choice of technology, whether it be the labor saving or labor using type. The labor saving type uses capital to replace labor. The consequence is that $\frac{dN}{dK}$ is negative and so is the indirect effect. This labor saving type of technology is common in the United States, where automation may be a major objective. Labor-using technology, on the other hand, operates so that the more capital is used, the more labor will be employed. There is complementarity between capital and labor. In a labor-using technology, $\frac{dN}{dK}$ is positive, and so is the indirect effect of capital. The Japanese have a large, well-trained labor supply, and they seem to prefer the labor using technology to accentuate the indirect effect of capital.

The third element is that, since it is difficult to keep the growth of income on the equilibrium expansion path, a higher growth rate than the equilibrium rate is preferred to a lower rate. The evil of inflation is preferred to that of recession. The next question is, how have the Japanese managed to accomplish this?

The high savings ratio is maintained through a number of institutional devices. In general, workers tend to save less than capitalists—not only because they have a low level of income, but also because they are not as familiar with efficient investment opportunities as are capitalists. Japan has maintained a rather low labor share of the national income. Further, it is not clear whether the labor share has recently been rising or falling. (If "labor" refers to nonagricultural labor, its share of the national income is rising. If farmers are included, however, the labor share of the national income is falling.) The labor force is paid wages and bonuses. There are two big semi-annual bonuses at New Year's and at Mid-Summer Day (July 7th.) Consumption is determined by wages, which are kept low; savings come largely from bonuses which are quite large. Japan has a primitive consumer credit system. In order to buy expensive or durable items, the Japanese initially have to save more than do Americans. In the interior of Japan, for instance, there are tremendous numbers of little family-operated businesses and farms with very small capital and practically no credit. These people have to save a great deal for expansion, if they have any ambition at all.

Yet the Japanese have a very favorable tax treatment of interest and dividends which we do not. This favorable tax treatment of property income is an incentive for even the working man to save. Taxes on dividends are paid separately from other income taxes and at low rates. Furthermore, certain categories of stocks can be held in anonymous accounts to avoid taxes.

Finally, the Japanese economy, despite the fact that it has no defense budget, is inflating even faster than ours. The way for the public to beat inflation is to accumulate earning assets such as stocks of land. Consequently, the Japanese system tends to operate in favor of a high savings ratio not only for workers, farmers, and property owners, but also for corporations.

How do the Japanese keep the capital-output ratio low or the productivity of capital high? They concentrate their investments on directly productive facilities, namely, plants and factories. They neglect housing. As a consequence, the housing situation in Japan is bad, and is deteriorating day by day. The Japanese neglect public works. Any public building, a university building particularly, that is more than two years old, looks like a shack. Public safety is also neglected, with the consequence of frequent landslides and floods. Japan has the world's worst pollution problems. Americans were alerted to the problem of mercury poisoning by the Japanese, who were the first to encounter such difficulty. The basic reason for all of these problems is that money goes so largely to plants and factories.

How have the Japanese been able to maintain high labor productivity? An increasing part of the labor force is educated. Formerly the average Japanese secured only a compulsory education of eight years. Now compulsory education has been extended to nine years, and in addition, more and more Japanese are going to college just as in the United States. However, the Japanese education system is putting too much emphasis on applied sciences. The government is trying to shock the system into a line of education aimed directly at economic productivity. The Japanese student is discouraged from studying law, literature or philosophy, for which the qualifying examinations are difficult. If he wants to go into business or engineering, however, the examinations are somewhat easier. The Japanese teachers' union (which happens to be dominated by Communists) is fighting this change tooth and nail.

The Japanese are also putting women to work much more effectively than they have in the past. Formerly the female labor force was largely occupied serving tea to the male labor force. But now women work along side of men at more meaningful jobs.

There is no craft unionism in Japan. All unions are industrial unions. The significance of the difference is that workers can be easily transferred from job to job without jurisdictional difficulties.

Workers are shifting out of agriculture where their productivity is low. Not only are large numbers of workers transferring out, but the more effective ones are doing so. The unpaid family force, which used to be about a third of the total Japanese labor force, has now been reduced to a tenth. Agriculture in Japan tends to be put increasingly into the hands of the Mamma, the Grandma and the Grandpa of the family, while the "prime-age male" has gone to the factory. The Japanese are also doing a better job than Americans in building factories in the small towns to make use of the spare time of farmers in the nearby countryside.

The Japanese system is not really of the free enterprise type; it is a guided economy, using what the French call "indicative planning." Japanese production is much more nearly risk-free than is American. "Indicative planning" means that the Japanese government has a plan which anticipates what every industry should accomplish. If a producer firm acts in accordance with the plan, financing is made available to it at a low interest rate. (Monetary policy is much more heavily relied upon than is fiscal policy.) Suppose, however, that the plan turns out to be wrong and a firm has overexpanded: it is not placed in jeopardy because government assistance will be forthcoming. The only instance in which a firm suffers the loss, and government assistance is not extended, is when the products of the firm do not meet specified physical requirements.

The Japanese economy is designed primarily for growth, but it is not ideal from the viewpoint of equitable distribution of income. The labor share of national income is low. Public works and services are neglected, and a large share of the national income goes to property owners, dividend receivers, and capital providers. Although these people are generously rewarded, they are not responsible for major business decisions, which are largely made by the government.

What are some of the problems that the Japanese are facing? One is the question of whether they will be able to maintain their rapid economic growth. Where will the additional labor supply come from? It is doubtful whether it will be possible for the Japanese to keep on improving their labor supply by recruiting women for production and transferring farmers to factories. Will they import workers from Taiwan, Korea, or other Asian countries? One cannot overlook the fact that there is animosity between the Japanese and these people. The Japanese have been borrowing technology from the West. Will not this backlog be eventually exhausted? The Japanese have just about caught up now?

How much longer can the Japanese continue the strategy of concentrating their resources on directly productive facilities? The people are demanding housing, school buildings, safety devices, and anti-pollution measures. There have been pressures for the improvement of the social security system. (The Japanese health care plan is better than ours, but their old-age and unemployment insurance systems are much worse.) There have been pressures from the United States for Japan to spend more on defense. Can the Japanese government withstand these pressures and keep on pushing for economic growth? What should be the choice in the trade-off between economic growth and other objectives?

Another problem facing Japan is that she does not have any raw materials worth mentioning. She needs imports and, consequently, must promote exports. Her main export market is the United States. What would happen to Japan if the United States should have a recession, or adopt protectionistic policies under the pressure of American business and labor unions?

The Japanese are talking about closer trade relations with the Soviet Union and with Red China. (Of course, it would not be the first time that a country changed its political leanings when its economic interests so dictated.) I do not know whether this trade realignment would be an improvement. Nor am I convinced that the Japanese system is any sort of a model for the rest of the world. But I do recognize some of the desirable features in the Japanese system for economic growth—whether that system evolved by chance or by design.

REFERENCES

1. R. F. Harrod, "An Essay on Dynamic Theory," *Economic Journal* (March 1939).

2. The easiest presentation is, however, E. D. Domar, "Expansion and Employment," *American Economic Review* (March 1947).

3. I have tried to spell this point out in a recent article: "The Japanese Growth Path: Stable or Unstable?" published in English in a Japanese journal, *Keizai Kenkyū* (April, 1970).

4. The neo-Cambridge or neo-Keynesian School, particularly Mrs. Joan Robinson, disagrees, on the ground that "capital" and its productivity are both meaningless and non-measurable, in a regime of heterogeneous capital goods. See G. C. Harcourt, "Some Cambridge Controversies in the Theory of Capital," *Journal of Economic Literature* (June 1969), and Joan Robinson, *Economic Philosophy* (London: Watts, (1962), Chi. iii, esp. p. 68 f.